Mantra Yoga

Jairam Seshadri has been practising Mantra Yoga for over 30 years and considers himself as nothing but for his mantras and prayers. Raised in India, he worked for several decades as an accountant in senior positions in North America. He founded the School of Wisdom in Toronto that made the eternal principles of Vedanta and Sanatana Dharma accessible to the Western mind. Jairam currently lives in Chennai, the place of his birth.

Mantra Yoga

HOW TO INCREASE
YOUR INNER POWER AND POTENTIAL

JAIRAM SESHADRI

RUPA

Published by
Rupa Publications India Pvt. Ltd 2021
7/16, Ansari Road, Daryaganj
New Delhi 110002

Sales centres:
Allahabad Bengaluru Chennai
Hyderabad Jaipur Kathmandu
Kolkata Mumbai

ISBN: 978-93-90918-48-5

First impression 2021

10 9 8 7 6 5 4 3 2 1

The moral right of the author has been asserted.

Printed at Saurabh Printers Pvt. Ltd, Noida

*This book is dedicated to the memory of
His Holiness Swami Sivananda Maharaj of Rishikesh
(1887–1963), founder of the Divine Life Society.*

CONTENTS

PROLOGUE

In a wonderful excerpt from a short story titled 'The Nine Billion Names of God' (which even elicited a charming response from the present Dalai Lama when it was published over 50 years ago), Arthur C. Clarke wrote of a Tibetan Lama, who presented himself to a successful American electronics entrepreneur with a strange request. The Lama wished to acquire the latest automatic sequence Mark V computer. The engineer was bewildered at this request from a self-professed ascetic, living in the deserted plains of Tibet, for a computer that was one of the most technologically advanced. With due deference, he requested to know the reason for such an acquisition. The Lama explained that for the past three centuries, the Lamasery, from the very time that it was founded, had been compiling all the possible names of God. He said:

All the many names of the Supreme Being—God, Jehovah, Allah, and so on—are only man-made labels. Our Lamasery has devised a unique alphabet and among all the possible combinations of letters in this unique alphabet, devised solely for this purpose, there are, what one may call, the real names of God.

The Lama and his brethren, over generations, by systematic permutation of the letters of their alphabet, had been trying to list them all, starting at AAAAAAAA and working up to ZZZZZZZZ. Buried in that gargantuan list, according to the Lama, would be the genuine names of God. The Lama stated that with the currently slow progress, he expected it to take them about 15,000 years to complete the task.

'But with the help of the Mark V, the process would be cut short to about a week.'

Astounded by the tale, the computer engineer, nevertheless, personally agreed to deliver the computer and volunteered to oversee Project Shangri-La (as it came to be dubbed) in a remote part of Tibet.

It was during the fourth or fifth day there that they learned through a reliable source, close to the Lama, the real purpose behind the project. According to this source, once all the names were listed (the Lamas had estimated there were, in total, nine billion names of God) the purpose of life, as we know it, would have been fulfilled. The human race, they had pointed out, will have finished what it was created to do, and there would not be any point in carrying on, upon which God would simply step in and wind things up.

Or so they believed.

The source went on to add his own opinion that, on the chance that God does not simply step in and wind things up, they will blame the computer and all hell will break loose. The lamas will begin to vent their anger on the engineers on the pretext of divine retribution.

All this made the engineers very nervous and they were just glad that they had a couple of days before the end of the computer-run to ruminate and arrange a quick flight out of that remote hinterland, having no option but to believe it would be 'in the nick of time'.

And so, it turned out, that the engineers found themselves striding briskly towards the tarmac, where the pristine figure of a DC-10 was standing to haul them away to safety, at the final hour of the computer-run.

The engineers had no intention of finding out whether the Mark V stood up to its legendary reputation. They were not even waiting to find out what those nine billion names of God were or for that matter even one name of God. They had never walked out on a job before, but they had no qualms about doing so now. They were thankful that they would not be around to 'face the music' that was sure to ensue, from the Lamasery.

As they strode, their brisk strides collectively turned into a quick trot towards the plane, fear propelling their movement forward. As they did so, one of the engineers realized, looking at his watch, that the Mark V should have completed its run at about that very moment.

With a sigh of relief, he looked up at the night sky, perhaps, grateful, that he would soon be hauled away to safety.

And what he saw in the pressing dark sky above made him stop in his tracks and call weakly to his compatriots, asking them, too, to look above.

All of them noticed that overhead, without any fuss, the stars were going out, one by one!

IN SEARCH OF THE
ENLIGHTENED ONE

By Jairam Seshadri

In search of the Enlightened One trudged the Little One
Of the Master, with a nimbus hallowed, golden,
The One with only a staff and a pot to his name,
Yet with a wealth far greater than any can claim.

The Enlightened One, whose words soothe the soul so,
Whose mellow glance alone raises downed moods so,
Mountainous presence, from within a misty calm,
Deep shadowy silence wafting wisteria, a dreamy balm.

To the One who keenly dissolves multiplicities,
The Little One ploughed through villages and cities,
Through hills, dales, cavernous rocky harsh trails,
Dark infested jungles, even through the epicentre of wails.

Treading miles of ground, plateaus, stone-dry, parched,
Barefoot, his amniotic feet cracked and starched,
Through deserts with only sand-dunes, the torrid sun,

To accompany, clinging alone, the thought of the One.

Leaner by the day and caring less for looks vain,
Withering away, further any personal gain,
His mien ash-smeared, years of sheen collecting
Within his spirit-frame, all pillars of attachment crumbling.

With not a single outward glance in his advance,
Other than to be in the Enlightened One's presence,
Too, now with only a staff, a pot to his frame,
All other behind, whispering the hallowed One's name.

With mind solely on the One riveting,
His thoughts crystal, sparks around him, prayers, forming
Cravings carelessly into the ether effervescing,
Leaving a laser-like, for the One alone pining.

The Little One, little no more, no fervour diminishing,
Despite all hope dimming of ever finding
The Enlightened One, touching skies, no hint of canker,
The elements about, all embracing, wishing closer.

Now placidly, solely, serenely in the Now,
With no thought even of the One he wished to bow,
When once stooping to a crystal, a mere, to quench a thirst,
Sees a reflection, his own, glowing and aburst.

A silvery beard, hair a halo, moonlit white,
An aura reflected, beyond, no mere sprite,
Eyes pools of delving compassion, a caressing hue,
Deep murmur, reverberating to the depths of the cosmic pool.

Oftentimes, in solitude, when in peace, you breathe,
You, the Breather, the Breath, One—no duality,
Or when watching a dancer weaving her intricate dance,
As in a trance, try telling the dancer from the dance.

Chapter 1

THE FOUNDATION

Mantras are those invocations, often in a language quite alien. They are often chanted in yoga classes or by monks clad in saffron robes. The words tumble out, sounding like marbles rattling in a tin can. The invocations seem to have no rational basis and are for the most part, dismissed out of hand.

Not so fast!

The aim of this book is to show that there is a rational basis for chanting mantras and that the path outlined in the discipline involved in Mantra Yoga helps in attaining one's higher states.

The Four Main Yogas in Relation to Mantra Yoga

It is well known that the word 'yoga' means 'union' or 'to yoke with' and it refers to the union of our present state of mind with our higher states. It would be more apt to say that the present state dissolves into higher states.

There are four main yogas, four main paths that lead to enlightenment or Shanti:

1. Karma Yoga—The path that helps in attaining one's higher states through service or work that ultimately benefits humanity rather than merely just oneself.

2. Bhakti Yoga—The path that leads to one's higher state through devotion and pure love.

3. Raja Yoga—The path that leads to one's higher states through mysticism, meditation and concentration. Hatha Yoga also forms part of Raja Yoga.

4. Jnana Yoga—The path that leads to one's higher states through intellectual means, through rationalization.

These four paths may be distinct. Yet all these four yogas are intricately and inextricably intertwined with each other. Aspirants do not—cannot—follow one path exclusively to reach their higher states. They follow all four paths with one path or another predominating, according to their nature, in their quest to attain enlightenment or Shanti.

Mantra Yoga is the path of attaining one's higher states through chanting of mantras. It is an integral part of the four yogas but is especially close to Bhakti Yoga, the path of devotion to a particular ideal or deity as the mantras themselves, as we will learn, are related to particular deities. Although this is generally true, there are mantras that are associated not with any deity but with the formless Infinite Spirit for those who are not inclined to worship any particular deity with form. However, it is important to bear in mind that the discipline of Mantra Yoga incorporates the four main Yogas in its quest to attain the state of Shanti. It does this through meditation (Raja Yoga), the regular and sincere act of chanting mantras (Karma Yoga), love of the mantra and the deity that presides over each mantra (Bhakti Yoga) and understanding the rationale behind the chanting of mantras (Jnana Yoga).

The act of chanting mantras to attain higher states requires a certain discipline. That discipline has a scientific and rational basis. If the rationale and the processes are not understood or known, one could easily end up questioning and doubting the act of chanting mantras. On the other hand, if we are armed with a measure of understanding of the reasons and the rationale behind the process, our commitment will be that much more.

This book attempts to do just that by examining the discipline required in practising Mantra Yoga. Faith, as we will learn in the coming chapters, should never be blind.

Having said that, let us move forward in laying the foundation for learning the intricacies of Mantra Yoga.

A Mantra Is a Mantra because...

Although the word 'mantra' is a Sanskrit word, the tradition of chanting mantras is not exclusive to the East. Every religion has mantras that are considered sacred and are repeated by the devout.

In Hinduism, a mantra is deemed to be a mantra only after individuals have succeeded in attaining their higher states upon chanting it. For example, individuals have attained enlightenment by regularly and sincerely chanting the mantra '*Om Namaha Shivaya*', which merely translates to 'Salutations to Lord Shiva.' This mantra is as old as the Vedas. (The Vedas are sacred texts of the Hindu religion and some experts claim they are over 7,000 years old.) Several such mantras from antiquity have remained relevant to date and are not lost to obscurity. The fact that they have survived the test of time may not, on that fact alone, prove their efficacy and potency but it should, at the very least, be one reason not to dismiss them offhand.

The Nature of Pleasure

We have learned that a deemed mantra has a certain proven potency. Let us begin the process of learning about what is involved in Mantra Yoga from the very beginning, for, after all, it is a very good place to start.

Let us begin by asking the question: what is it that enjoins us to act, to do anything in this world?

Is not the answer to this question 'pleasure'? That and 'fear of pain'. We tend to always gravitate towards committing acts that will lead to pleasure or acts that make us flee from pain.

In our quest to attain higher states, it would therefore behoove us to understand the nature of 'pleasure'. 'Pleasure' and 'pain' are the two catalysts that enjoin us to commit to any act in this world. So let us delve a little deeper into the nature of pleasure.

For starters, we know that pleasure, as with every pleasing experience, has 'diminishing marginal utility', to borrow a term from economics. To illustrate, if we are indulging in a chocolate-eating binge, every additional chocolate bar consumed will bring lesser satisfaction than the piece of chocolate eaten before, till we arrive at a point when the mere thought of eating chocolate disgusts us. So, too, for life's pleasures pursued as ends in themselves.

But 'pleasure' has a more sinister, a more deadly effect if not recognized for what it is.

'Pleasures' are ephemeral, they are transient by definition. If indulged in wantonly, they lead to an incessant craving, for they can never be permanently quenched. 'Lust' and 'greed for wealth' are two prime examples of such pleasure that are only temporarily quenched each time they are indulged in. Sexual pleasure within the confines of true love, on the other hand, can be a means to regulating this particular desire and by doing so, such pleasures can serve as a stepping stone to our higher states. Outside of true love, however, sexual pleasure, merely to satiate lust, will only lead to greater lust, acting like an addictive drug.

Pursuing ephemeral pleasures as ends in themselves, renders us slaves to such pleasures. But human beings are not meant to be slaves, especially of our own desires. We are born to master our internal and external worlds.

Even our reflexive instincts that seem to be a part of our hardwired personality, those instincts that seem quite apart from any conscious decision-making, can be transcended. This ability to not remain slaves to our instincts and bodily needs, in essence, separates the human kingdom from the animal kingdom.

Pleasures, therefore, should not be pursued for the sake of pleasures alone, but as stepping stones to growth and ultimately to the state of enlightenment.

Pleasure and Pain Are Two Sides of the Same Coin

Merely living life for the sake of pleasure alone will ultimately bring greater pain. Pleasures, as ends in themselves (and not as stepping stones for growth), will result in greater suffering. This is because we are investing in a cause that is transient; dwelling on and desiring anything transient is a lost cause. When the pleasure we seek has passed on, pain will follow, for pleasure and pain are two sides of the same coin. Pleasure, without an equal measure of pain in some form, is not possible.

Without consciously recognizing that pleasure and pain are the obverse and reverse sides of the same coin, we are left to the vicissitudes of craving for pleasure, experiencing pain and, in the process, regressing to enslaving ourselves to our own desires. However, if we begin to look upon pleasure and pain as stepping stones to higher growth, we begin to focus on the subtler, eternal aspects of our own personalities, and we will slowly begin to shed our craving for pleasure.

To top it all, using 'pleasure and pain' as stepping stones to a higher, more subtle state, gives meaning to life, more so than merely craving pleasure and fleeing from pain, which is reflective of a knee-jerk lifestyle, without evolving to higher states that transcend the need for pleasure and the fear of pain.

As an aside, Lord Shiva, it is said, annihilated all desire for pleasure, burning them to ashes. That is why Shiva is usually depicted as being smeared in ashes. Lord Shiva is a state of being, our higher state that has conquered the need for pleasure and indeed the fear of pain.

This Relative World

More importantly, though, the pleasure one feels is almost always defined relative to the pleasure felt in the company we keep. Pleasure is almost never an absolute experience.

What do we mean?

Well, any pleasure we feel is relative to how others are feeling. The pleasure we feel may also be compared to pleasure derived from a similar or the same act performed by us earlier.

To illustrate, the thrill, the over-the-moon feeling of winning a million-dollar lottery, would vanish instantly if every soul on this planet also won a million dollars. The market would adjust and our purchasing power would remain the same as before. Our balloon would burst.

If, however, you are one of the chosen few (or better, the only one) to have won the million dollars, you will experience a genuine high. As cruel as it may seem then, your joy on wining the million dollars is at the 'expense' of those who have not won the lottery; your joy rests and rides on the backs of all those who were not lucky enough to have won the lottery.

And so, sadly, in this world, our happiness or unhappiness is almost always defined in relative terms—relative to the happiness or unhappiness of others in our particular orbit. If others are relatively less happy, we are, by definition, happier.

Schadenfreude, a German word meaning the delight that comes from the discomfiture and unhappiness faced by others, speaks about the nature of this relative world. The more enmeshed in the relative world we are, the more of a relative 'happiness' we feel, when others are not as well off.

A cartoon in *The New Yorker* magazine depicted this thought brilliantly:

Two dogs in a bar are having a drink.
One dog is telling the other: 'It is not enough that we should succeed. Cats must also fail.'

Any happiness or pleasure that is measured by the level of happiness in others—the possible smugness that might arise seeing the discomfiture in others—can never give rise to peace within. This is because this kind of pleasure is dependent on the relative state of others. This is important, even critical, to understand. Any pleasure or happiness that rests on, or is dependent on others who do not enjoy the same level of happiness or pleasure, will never last long, will never give rise to peace within. Dependency is a state that does not flow from within; it is a state that is subject to factors not within our control. Pleasures experienced in the relative world, therefore, are never genuine, they are artificial in their very nature, being dependent as they are on factors outside.

Any dependence, therefore, is a form of enslavement.

The State of Shanti

The relative world, as we know, is characterized by experiences that fall within a spectrum. For example, at the opposite ends of the spectrum lie attributes such as pleasure–pain, joy–misery, happiness–unhappiness, black–white, fat–thin, beautiful–ugly and so on—opposites that pervade all aspects of our life. There are, of course, several shades of each experience in between each opposite end. With this in mind, there is one point that we need to be consciously aware of. And that is:

Every attribute exists only because its opposite exists.

Every attribute?

Yes! That is the very nature of this relative world we live in. Every attribute exists only because its opposite attribute exists—they are codependent.

In other words, if there were no ugliness whatsoever, there would be no 'beautiful' whatsoever! If there was no misery experienced by us, where would the concept of joy be? No one would know what being 'joyous' would mean if no misery were experienced by human beings.

To further clarify this, consider the mundane compliment: 'You're the most beautiful girl I have seen!' In this statement, there is an implication that other girls are not as beautiful, even if only in the eyes of the one giving the compliment. In a single stroke, the statement condemns all others to a lesser state of beauty in comparison.

The Paradox of 'Absolute' Happiness

Having proven that all attributes exist in relation to their opposites, there now arises a paradox that is critical to comprehend if we are to move forward in understanding and inculcating the process and the discipline of Mantra Yoga in our lives.

And that paradox is: how do we pursue our own happiness without depending on the level of happiness of others? Or, to put it another way, how do we remain happy, independent of external conditioning, such as, perhaps, the ever-increasing material riches of those whom we relate to?

The answer is a revelation: it introduces us to a new state that is unknown to most of us. To gain awareness of the new state, imagine that the opposite states of pleasure and pain are hovering just above our right and left eyes, respectively. Remember, you cannot just have pleasure hovering above your right eye without pain hovering somewhere very near, for they exist in relation to each other. They are two sides of the same coin—you cannot have one without the other! Remember, too, that we always seek or gravitate towards pleasure and avoid or flee from pain.

Then the answer to the question 'how can we remain independent and pursue our own happiness without diminishing the happiness of others?' lies in simply becoming aware of and attaining a state that hovers above (transcends) these two states of pleasure and pain. This state eternally hovers above us like a golden orb, hovers continually above the twin opposites of pleasure–pain.

This state that hovers above pleasure and pain has a name: it is the state of Shanti. It is this state that should be the goal of life. For, after attaining this state, we can achieve our material goals with greater ease and efficiency. Attaining this state of Shanti entitles us to a life of calmness and peace that cannot be articulated. Mantra Yoga transports us to that rarefied state.

Seek Ye First the State of Shanti

Jesus said: 'Seek ye first the Kingdom of God.'

He did not tell us to seek the kingdom of God after making our first million dollars, or after establishing our first start-up, or after finding the love of our lives or after raising a family.

He tells us to seek Shanti first. Our priorities in life become clearer when we do; our inherent and unique strengths are revealed to us; we can pursue our passions with a view to achieving goals; indeed, our passions are made clearer to us. And when we pursue our goals from a state of Shanti, our efforts consciously and coincidentally benefit humanity.

Jesus Christ is known as the 'Prince of Peace', the 'Prince of Shanti'. He was not, nor ever claimed to be, the 'Prince of Happiness'. He would have shunned and pitied those who worshiped him as the 'Prince of Pleasure', as pleasure is enmeshed in the relative world. What is 'rich and pleasurable' for some, may not be so for another. Christ's inner peace was independent of how others felt.

The Buddha was known as 'The Awakened One'—awakened to the peace within, not to unsurpassed material riches that would keep him awake in frantic frenzy.

The state of Shanti transcends the relative world. The only opposite to Shanti is the relative world and all that characterizes this world.

Inner peace or Shanti, a state that transcends relative opposites, is attainable by human beings, independent of how well-off materially they are or the company they keep are.

There is a Zen Koan, that illustrates this particular point well, and it is posed in the form of a question and answer:

Question: Who uttered the Buddha's name?
Answer: The Buddha uttered the Buddha's name.

That is so because all of us have the potential to awaken to that state of Shanti, to be Buddhas in our own right. It is this state alone that will transport us to the state of oneness and compassion, a state that enables peace to flow from within, and not from material riches without. Material wealth is subject to change, deplete, dry up, vanish.

If we remain enmeshed in the relative world, we wear the cloak of separateness from others and even from our own selves! We identify ourselves as distinct and separate from others. The state of feeling separate, the conviction that as individuals, we are distinct, discrete entities, leads to competition (and inner conflict and emotional problems), which when taken to its extreme, leads to jealousy, hatred, depression, even resulting in the most heinous of crimes.

We are all one in essence. When oneness pervades, there can be no negative thoughts. Shanti is that state of enlightenment. The state of Shanti unites us all. It is up to us individually to realize that state.

The next chapter delves into the nature of the state of Shanti, the importance of faith and how faith and knowledge act as the two wings of an aspirant in following the discipline of Mantra Yoga.

Om=Om=Om

Chapter 2

THE STATE OF SHANTI DEFINED

Why Define the State of Shanti?

Let us now try and define a term used often, not only in this book but in every scripture: enlightenment or the state of Shanti.

Why is it important to define the term?
In any journey, it is critical to know and to clearly define the destination.

Where are we headed?
This is a question we must clearly answer!

If we are not clear as to where we are headed and why we are headed there, any lack of clarity will compel us to continually look over our shoulders, doubting the path we are taking.

Why are we undertaking this journey of chanting mantras every day?
If the answer to this is abstract, foggy, wishy-washy, asking us

to rely on blind faith, it may render every step we take to be futile! So, visualization and absolute clarity of the end result are critical for success in any endeavour.

The end result, in our case, is the state of Shanti.

Defining Shanti or enlightenment, and clearly visualizing the state, helps our subconscious and conscious minds to focus and guide us.

Mantra Yoga is the vehicle that transports us to that state and in order to be committed to, and fully engaged with, riding that vehicle, we need to be crystal clear as to what this state of Shanti is and how we would feel if and when we do reach that state. Would it be worth it? How would it affect our personality? Will we be devoid of every misery after having attained the state of Shanti?

We need to answer these questions in order to get a feel for the state of Shanti that will give us added focus to the practice and discipline of Mantra Yoga.

If the state of Shanti is not appealing to a spiritual aspirant, the aspirant will not practise Mantra Yoga with as dedicated a zeal as as aspirant to whom it is appealing.

The State of Shanti: What It Is Not

Before attempting to reveal the nature of the state of Shanti, let us be clear on what it is not.

At the outset, attaining the state of Shanti does not mean we will be free from problems. Being free from problems and leading a stress-free life is not ideal for life, in general, anyway! In a study of the evolution of biological organisms, those that experience no stress become extinct. If you do not use it, you lose it. Those organisms who are stress-free lose the ability to adapt to changing circumstances and overcome hurdles. Stress is what keeps the survival instinct in fine fettle and tuned. So a stress-free life is not healthy, not conducive to a good life. Stress that is manageable is important for growth.

Nor does attaining the state of Shanti mean that we will be privy to supernatural powers. There are, no doubt, individuals with special powers and the mere presence of supernatural powers does not necessarily mean those who possess them are enlightened. On the contrary, they may live in morbid fear of losing those very powers and are voluntarily holding themselves ransom to jealousy, anger and other negative influences. All these negative traits, you might recall, are of the relative world.

The State of Shanti: What Is It?

The human mind, more than the minds of any other species, is creative enough and capable of adapting to varying and trying circumstances. We are also aware that the human mind, if left to freely and wantonly follow its cravings for pleasure, will bring much suffering in its wake.

The state of Shanti, though, is more than merely the ability to adapt and overcome hurdles and tragedies. Shanti is a state that looks upon pleasure and pain with an equal measure of calmness, even indifference. It is this measure of equanimity towards the two prime catalysts of life's activities that gives those in the state of Shanti the ability to deal with vicissitudes and tragedies (that almost invariably occur in life) with resolve, calmness and fortitude.

The state of Shanti transcends all opposites of the relative world, displaying a resolute stillness and clarity when pressing problems confront us, without succumbing to fear, anger, hatred. It enables one to face life with cheer and grace, whatever the circumstances.

At the risk of repetition, the state of Shanti enables one to see things for what they truly are and gives one the ability to deal with them effectively in a clinical manner. Shanti enables one to accept fortune and misfortune with an equal eye, for the one in the state of Shanti is wise enough to know that experiencing joy at the sight of fortune will also mean experiencing misery when fortune passes on or does a 'no-show'.

More importantly, Shanti induces in us the dawning of acceptance and the ability to live in harmony with the environment as well true contentment, shunning the very notion of greed and acquisitiveness.

In the state of Shanti, the knowledge that pleasure and pain are two sides of the same coin is second nature; Shanti gives one the ability to rebound faster from setbacks and be less affected by the tentacles of suffering than those enmeshed in the relative world. This, however, also means that we are liberated from the need for pleasure, the craving for 'good times' that, for some, defines status; liberated from the desire for name, fame and from seeking recognition from others for our well-being.

This, in essence, defines the state of Shanti.

Rather mundane, no, this state of Shanti? Is that all there is to Shanti? Perhaps, but a mundane state that is miraculous. A cheerful, miraculous mundane!

We humans are very intelligent creatures and the fact that we are at the top of the pecking order is self-evident. Some, however, would debate the fact whether we are the most wise!

It is this aspect that the state of Shanti addresses. Mantra Yoga, by helping us attain an unshakeable serenity within, gives us the ability to live a full life in an exalted state of oneness with all. We can only achieve our cherished goals when we are calm and cheerful and nurture an abiding faith in our own selves regardless of whatever life may throw at us.

Yes, Shanti also gives us an unshakeable faith in ourselves!

The Importance of Faith

Faith is critical in this process. One has to believe.

Faith, though, has connotations of blind belief. The subtle distinction between faith and blind belief must be understood. When faith is spoken of in the context of Mantra Yoga, it is never blind faith but 'reasoned' faith.

To illustrate, we study a road map (created by someone of whom we know little of) when we wish to reach an unknown destination. Or we board a plane and entrust our lives to a pilot (again, of whom we know little of). Both acts are performed on faith. Faith, here, may well rest on the knowledge that many before us have relied on that road map and many have boarded that plane, all of whom have reached their destinations successfully. This is faith based on the knowledge that we know how maps are made and that there are strict regulations for airlines to adhere to safety standards. This is faith that is reasonable, faith that is sensible. In contrast, imagine boarding a spaceship that had suddenly landed in your backyard and entrusting aliens to ferry you to your choice of destination! Now, that would be blind faith.

Faith in Mantra Yoga need not be blind. True, scores of individuals have not trod the Mantra Yoga path on a daily basis and fewer still have attained enlightenment; it certainly is not an everyday event, not as routine as boarding a commercial airline and flying to your destination. The spiritual path has never been embraced by too many. The allure of the tentacles of pleasure are far too intoxicating to rationalize its transience. Only a few, who are willing to walk the 'razor's edge', are apt to stop and question themselves hurtling towards pleasure at any instance. The path to Shanti is, after all, very subtle, esoteric, not meant for everyone. Over time, more aspirants will recognize the value of treading the path. But the fact that there are very few such individuals in the past should not detract us from studying its validity, as those who have trod the Mantra Yoga path sincerely, have attained the state of Shanti. If we wish to grow in faith in this process and reach enlightenment (our destination), it is up to us to diligently study and see whether the efforts of these few and rare individuals were futile or fruitful.

One of the requirements of faith is, at times, to question our senses. This may seem illogical, for the senses are our gateways to direct perception and experience. In questions of science, Galileo said, the authority of a thousand is not worth the humble reasoning of a single individual. However, it is also wise to realize that all that we see or feel through the senses may not be true. For example, when we look up at the sky during the daytime, we do not see any stars. Does that mean there are no stars? When we look at a spoon immersed in a glass of water, it seems bent or broken. That does not mean that the spoon is actually bent or broken. Science explains that refraction bends light and, therefore, the spoon seems bent. In the same manner, we would do well to discriminate between what we are subconsciously attracted to through our senses and that which is the way of the wise. To discriminate between the lure of the senses (which is transitory) and the eternal requires a pure intellect, and it is this pure intellect that sheds light on the science of Mantra Yoga.

Doubts Are Angels

As we progress through life while holding on to the hemline of faith, questions and doubts will arise, assailing, battering, weakening our resolve to stay the course. It is then that we need to grow in knowledge, rectify the imbalance and through that, grow all the more in faith.

So bless those doubts that come!

Welcome them and transcend them!

It is by overcoming those very doubts that we not only renew and redouble our faith but also grow in knowledge. If there is no doubt at the outset, there can be no faith. Faith rests on the fact that doubts exist. Indeed, faith is energized by overcoming those very doubts. The greater the doubt overcome, the greater one's faith, for we would have also grown in knowledge in overcoming that doubt.

A lack of faith, then, is merely a sign that it is time for us to grow all the more. They are feelers reminding us to grow further in knowledge by learning from people who chant mantras on a regular basis or by reading up on the lives of sages who attained enlightenment through chanting such mantras. Doubts that cause one's faith to flicker are angels, reminding us that further wisdom beckons and that the state of Shanti is that much closer. If, on the other hand, we choose to harbour doubts or leave them unattended and stray from our chosen path, it will lead to irregularity and insincerity in the path of Mantra Yoga, and eventually to our downfall. For, a lack of faith, left unattended for long, will result in abandoning one's spiritual path, leading to suffering. Pain endured for the sake of growth is of value; pain with no growth is unacceptable.

Faith is, after all, the essence of a human being. Machines and computers are programmed to function in a certain way and they do as they are told most of the time. Machines do not question their innate abilities. Human beings alone are beset with doubts and are capable of transcending their doubts, instincts and senses through faith. Human beings who do not overcome and transcend and live up to their potential are simply not responding to their own innate higher calling. If we choose not to overcome doubts and re-establish faith, we are consciously choosing to remain stagnant.

Stagnation Is the Only Sin There Is

Our minds or our personalities remaining stagnant does not mean we remain as is, maintaining status quo. A stagnant personality is an oxymoron, for, choosing to remain stagnant is choosing to regress. A stagnant personality always regresses.

This is because our personalities, whether we like it or not, are always dynamic. We are alive, after all! We cannot be like stones. So, there is always movement in our personalities, either evolving or regressing, never stagnant. We are never stationary in our thoughts, beliefs and values. They are either decaying or growing stronger. They are in a constant state of flux, for

movement and change are signs of life. Stagnation in one's
personality is an illusion, for thoughts spiral downward over
time, unless a conscious decision is made to grow. Watching
mindless TV shows all day long, being a couch potato day-in-
day-out, not devoting time to learning a new art or a science
will result ultimately in our personalities spiralling downward
till we reach a stage where we would have forgotten what
we knew. The downward journey will result in hitting a wall
that painfully reminds us of our follies and that growth is the
only way out of the mire. Even inanimate objects that stagnate
eventually decay and crumble. If we remain as we are without
a conscious effort to grow in mind, intellect and spirit, we will
regress, decay and fall apart.

Having stressed the importance of nurturing a 'reasoned'
faith as opposed to a blind faith and the importance of
continually and consciously seeking to grow one's mind,
intellect, spirit and even the body, it is relevant to point out
that chanting mantras even when the faith is weak will benefit
the aspirant.

How so?

Well, whether you have faith in an umbrella's ability to
shelter you from rain or not, using an umbrella when it rains
will shelter you. Whether you have faith that exercise and
eating right will lead to better health or not, eating right and
exercising will invariably lead to better health.

It is the same with Mantra Yoga.

Repeating a mantra, even without faith, will benefit
aspirants. Chanting mantras when doubts continue to persist
is blind faith or no faith at all. Chanting mantras with faith
borne of an intellectual understanding and an appreciation,

however, will help us maintain our sincerity, regularity and intensity, hastening our spiritual progress.

The nature of Shanti will become even more clear as we wade into the next chapter and learn about knowledge and faith, the two wings of spiritual aspirants as they make their way to the state of Shanti.

Om=Om=Om

Chapter 3

LIMITATIONS OF THE RATIONAL AND THE RATIONALE OF THE IRRATIONAL

In the previous chapter, we learned that it is critical to gain an understanding of the end result—the destination—while pursuing any goal. Shanti or enlightenment is our goal and attaining that state will mean being liberated from the need for pleasure and the fear of pain. We also learned that in our path towards Shanti, faith is critical and that a distinction between blind belief and faith must be recognized. While blind faith must be avoided, true faith in this path can only be maintained by overcoming doubts that will invariably beset any aspirant. Once doubts are overcome, it will only strengthen one's faith and so doubts should be looked upon as gateways to greater levels of awareness and knowledge. Doubts are opportunities for further growth towards Shanti.

Choosing to grow must be a conscious decision and the only decision that we must stick to at all costs. And 'growth' necessarily means growth towards the state of Shanti; growth cannot be towards any other goal as an end in itself. In other words, every material goal sought, must be used as a stepping stone to something more lasting, less transient, eternal. And that something is the state of Shanti.

Mantra Yoga aids in this growth and, as was pointed out, growth will occur if mantras are chanted even without faith; if, however, mantras are chanted with 'reasoned' faith (faith that is balanced with knowledge), the aspirant's practice will be that much more sincere and fruitful.

Ultimately Knowledge Can Only Take Us So Far

To reiterate, then, faith is critical and faith and knowledge should balance each other. They are the two wings of the bird flying towards Shanti.

At this stage it is important to mention that ultimately, knowledge will only take us up to a certain point, stopping short of the state of Shanti. In the realm of spirituality and in our march towards the state of Shanti, as much as we may continue to add to our knowledge, we will, at some point in our journey, say, 'I do not know beyond this, cannot see beyond that.' We will come to a point when we realize how little indeed we do know. For we are now in the realm of trying to define dimensions and states, which we are not fully equipped for.

To Define God Is to Defile God

We can define an object that is finite, one that we can touch, see, hear, feel, even if it is through electron microscopes, through the Hubble telescope or through robots that go the distance and land on Mars. We have visualized and determined how we should feel after attaining the state of Shanti. Defining the state of Shanti, though, will be an attempt to confine that state to the limited concepts of our mind. For our minds, by definition, are limited whereas the state of Shanti, transcends the senses. If we want, we can imagine a superior force, say 'God', dispensing the state of Shanti but we cannot possibly define God or say what or who He or She is. To do so, would be attempting to define the infinite; our senses and our minds, which are finite, will always fall short. Defining anything is subjecting it to the realm of our senses! How can God be within our limited senses?

At the very least, all we can do is to imagine and define how we would feel after attaining God (or the state of Shanti) in this very life, not after death. Note, we are not referring to states that we might or might not assume after death. Why? Because they cannot be proven. Mantra Yoga deals exclusively with states that we can experience in the here and now. And the state of Shanti can be experienced in this lifetime!

And yet, as we said, there will come a point when we, in our spiritual journeys, are compelled to say, 'From now on, it is all faith.' For knowledge, as one philosopher pointed out, is the finger that points us in the right direction, and does so only up to a certain point. After that point is reached, the finger disappears and faith alone carries us forward. When we reach that rarefied point when we do not feel the need to question and rationalize every step we take in this journey, we will no longer question our faith. We begin to know with conviction of a state that exists, that gives ineffable peace even if it still eludes us. We begin to realize the frailty and limitations of the human mind's ability to comprehend God and we simply chant mantras with full faith. However, to get to that point, beyond which the finger of knowledge disappears, we need to dispel doubts that surface, use the limited knowledge we have and the little faith bestowed on us to grow in faith and—yes—in knowledge!

It is somewhat like a flying fish. The flying fish propels itself above the water and flies above (transcends!) the water only by using the water it swims in. In the same manner, we must grow in knowledge and faith we are currently 'swimming in' to propel us to the state of Shanti, to a state that is ultimately independent of faith and knowledge. All of us, in our individually unique and uniquely individual spiritual journeys, will reach a stage when we echo Socrates and say 'how little we do know.' Bertrand Russell, too, pointed out that the trouble with the world is that the dim are overconfident and the bright are doubtful. It seems paradoxical to say that when the full realization of how little we do know dawns, we reach the threshold of wisdom. Yet, it is when we realize our senses are limited and come to rest on faith that we are, in effect, knocking on the doors of enlightenment or the state of Shanti.

The Rationale for Dimensions beyond Our Ken

We mentioned early on that there are realms and dimensions that our senses cannot comprehend, that are indeed beyond our ken, embodied as we are in a human body. This may seem farfetched to the rational mind. That's understandable. Again, it is not necessary to believe in other dimensions for the efficacy of Mantra Yoga to work. However, as stated earlier, to actually commit oneself to chanting on a regular basis requires a measure of understanding and faith in its efficacy. So, is there a way to understand and prove that dimensions beyond our ken are a distinct possibility?

We can attempt to do so initially, by taking one particular sense, say the sense of hearing. We hear sounds through our ears. Without trying to understand complex frequencies that will be briefly mentioned later, merely the knowledge that dogs can hear frequencies that human beings cannot shows that there are dimensions beyond humans' hearing ability. In the same way, there are dimensions beyond the normal human-seeing ken (for example, it has been scientifically proven that birds can see some ultraviolet frequencies that human beings cannot), which logically leads to the conclusion that there are indeed whole dimensions beyond a human being's limited holistic perception.

Science has proven that sound exists in four fundamental states. The first state we all know and hear easily—it is the dense audible state. The second state is a more refined state, which is inaudible to the physical ear. (Dogs are able to hear these refined frequencies that the human ear cannot.) The third state is a still higher, inner and more ethereal state where some can 'hear' others' thoughts through the vibrations that are created by thoughts, even when they are not in physical proximity. The more refined our mental state is, the more we are able to tune in to such thoughts. The fourth and final state of sound is the state that is undifferentiated from its very source. It's a form of energy and the very sound itself is one with the source of all energy, the very source of this universe. It is the primal cause. This classification has also been delineated in the Vedas which also mentions the word 'Om' from which all creation manifests.

In quantum physics, a quantum particle (a particle too

small for the human eye to see) can vanish without a trace or come into existence out of nowhere; it can move from one location to another without being anywhere in between; it can instantly flip from one state to another state. Now when scientists say the particle 'came into existence out of nowhere' 'without being anywhere in between' or 'without a trace', what they are saying is that our limited faculties (even with the tremendous technological advances that science has made) are not yet capable of comprehending all the dimensions there are in this universe. With the universe being infinite in the material and intellectual sense, there will, in all probability, always be aspects and dimensions that lie beyond our comprehension. Intellectually, it will be a continuous learning process, taking us ever closer, but never reaching, the threshold of God. Only by transcending the intellect and resting on faith can we attain God and the state of Shanti. And when we attain that state, silence alone will prevail.

As we go to the next chapter, it is helpful to bear in mind that faith and knowledge are, therefore, not contradictory; they support one another much more than we realize. This also lends credence to science and religion being complementary, rather than being at odds with each other. By strengthening the wing of knowledge (by explaining the rationale behind Mantra Yoga), the wing of faith is also strengthened. Thus, both faith in Mantra Yoga and the rationale behind Mantra Yoga will be nurtured and strengthened.

With this thought in mind, we will look at what the basics of Mantra Yoga are in the next chapter.

Om=Om=Om

Chapter 4

A MANTRA: ITS NUTS AND BOLTS

Before we begin analysing what a mantra is and what its parts are, we must always remember one thing. And that one thing is that Mantra Yoga is a verb. It is all very well to study the discipline required in the practice of Mantra Yoga, but they will remain in the realm of theory unless one practises the discipline of Mantra Yoga.

Bearing this in mind, let us familiarize ourselves with the parts of a mantra that all coalesce to give it its unique power.

Mantra–Its Etymological Derivation

'Mantra', as we know, is a Sanskrit word with two syllables. The first syllable, 'man', translates to 'mind'. The second syllable, 'tra' is derived from the root word 'trai', which means 'to protect'. So a mantra protects our minds and our thinking from negative thought and vibes. Another meaning attributed to 'tra' is 'to travel'. From this perspective, repetition of a mantra helps transport our minds to the realm that transcends the relative world and its world of opposites, to a state where limitations are not binding—the state of Shanti.

The Parts of a Mantra

A brief outline of the constituent parts of a mantra is helpful in understanding the concept and practise of Mantra Yoga. Before we list the parts that make up a mantra, we should know that the continued repetition of a mantra creates vibrations that are a form of energy. Repetition of a mantra, therefore, releases energy embedded in it.

Having said that, every mantra has six inherent attributes.

First, all mantras have a Deva or the presiding deity of the mantra. The Deva is the ultimate destination of the energy released from chanting the mantra. In other words, the Deva is the mantra's informing power. The energy within a mantra is also known as the *Sakti* (divine energy).

Second, all mantras have an interceding sage, who first attained enlightenment through the repetition of that mantra. The sage who, having first received the mantra through his austerities and powers borne of purity, bestowed the mantra on humanity. Sage Vishwamitra, for example, bestowed the Gayatri Mantra to humanity. He is the one who intercedes with Gayatri Devi for our cause (Gayatri Devi is one of the forms of the Divine Mother and the presiding deity of the Gayatri Mantra).

Third, every mantra has a Sakti embedded in the mantra, which is released when a mantra is chanted. This energy reaches the particular Deva associated with the mantra through the intercession of the presiding sage.

Fourth, all mantras have a *Bija* (seed) within which the Sakti is embedded. The inherent energy manifest in the mantra emanates from this seed. The Bija, then, is where the power of the mantra resides. It is its essence in the form of a particular word in the mantra. It is also known as the Bija-Akshara or the seed-word.

Fifth, all mantras have a *Killaka* (pillar or pin) which keeps the divine energy or the Sakti, plugged within the Bija of the mantra. The Killaka is unplugged only through constant and regular repetition of the mantra.

Finally, the mantra has a metre which governs the inflection of the voice. It is this metre that lends each mantra its unique vibrations.

This brief outline above will help in understanding some of the terms that will be used as we progress further. We should be able to come back to these six attributes as we gain familiarity with different mantras and learn the discipline and rationale of Mantra Yoga. So let us review the six parts of a mantra. They are:

(i) The presiding Deva or deity

(ii The sage who intercedes on our behalf with the presiding deity

(iii The Sakti or the divine energy

(iv) The Bija-Akshara or the seed-word within which the Sakti is embedded

(v) The Killaka that plugs the divine energy within the Bija-Akshara

(vi) A metre, unique to each mantra lending the mantra its unique sound vibrations

Mantra Yoga Is the Highest Form of Yagna

Any act that appeals to a higher power—prayer, worship, offering, sacrifice—is known as a *yagna* (pronounced 'yegg-nya'). The Bhagavad Gita states that of all the yagnas, Mantra Yoga is the highest form (Chapter 10, verse 25). The Gita uses the term Japa Yoga instead of the term Mantra Yoga. *Japa* simply means the repetition of a mantra.

It is time to remind ourselves here that the discipline of Mantra Yoga must necessarily incorporate the other yogas.

To sit down and chant mantras on a regular basis necessarily implies that our health is optimal. We know we cannot sit still for any length of time with a bad back or a weak constitution and so we need to practise Hatha Yoga or some set of physical exercises regularly.

To sit down and chant on a regular basis presupposes that we have the devotion and love (Bhakti Yoga) for chanting, without which our dedication to the art and sincerity to the cause will fall short.

It rests, too, on the foundation that we have rationalized the basis for such chanting (Jnana Yoga) or else our faith would falter.

It dictates that we follow a discipline and ultimately aim to benefit humanity (Karma Yoga) through our chanting.

And finally, concentration and meditation (Raja Yoga) are called for, born of an absence of fear to dive deep into the mystic realms within our minds.

Thus, we need to be physically, mentally and emotionally healthy to be able to chant mantras on a regular basis and, therefore, practising the other yogas together with Mantra Yoga is critical. As mentioned before, all yogas are interconnected and intertwined in the spiritual path to Shanti.

Name and Form Are One

Every mantra, as mentioned, has a presiding deity. Think of it as an image, a state, that is associated with that mantra. If we are chanting a particular mantra, we must make ourselves familiar with the deity or state associated with that mantra. (Usually, an aspirant chooses a mantra after gravitating towards a particular deity.) Since name and form are intricately connected, the chanting of the mantra (name) brings to mind the form of the deity. We can understand it in this way: mentioning the name of someone we know will immediately conjure up his or her form. Or by merely saying the word 'tree', for example, an image of a tree is conjured. If we see a picture of a tree, the word 'tree' surfaces in our minds.

It works both ways.

Name and form are, therefore, interconnected—think of one, the other immediately follows suit.

Mantra Yoga engages our bodies, our minds and our intellect and enables us to meditate on the form associated with the mantra. If the forms of Devas associated with particular mantras are not appealing to one's inclinations and we are more comfortable with the formless aspect of the Infinite, there are mantras that have the formless Infinite Spirit or Pure Light as their deity.

It is worth emphasizing that an infinite god with infinite compassion surely can have form and can also be formless. God will assume the form of our choosing as long as we are sincere and devoted to that form, even if it is a formless form! Do we not, as individuals, play different roles out of consideration for others? An individual may be a father, a husband, a friend, a brother, a master, a servant and so on. If one's nature, for example, is one in which the motherly instinct predominates and wishes to love God in the form of a child, God manifests accordingly, in the form of a child and devotees worship God in forms like baby Jesus and baby Krishna.

The Formless and the Diverse Forms, All Represent the One Infinite

A form is, however, often attributed to the formless Infinite Spirit, only so we human beings, who are with form, can relate to the Infinite Spirit in ways that are purely human.

There are five forms of a loving relationship between human beings, each of which has reached its supreme pinnacle between God and man in the annals of Hindu thought. The five forms of love and devotion we witness are:

(a) Love of a child for a father or mother
(b) Love and respect a servant has for a just and generous master
(c) Love between spouses
(d) Love a parent has for his or her child
(e) A serene calmness and peace felt in the presence of a guru

We can look upon the Infinite Spirit with a form as our parent, lover, guide, master or even our child. Some are able to relate to the formless Infinite Spirit in the same way, omnipotent, omniscient, omnipresent. One needs more imagination, however, for the Formless Spirit to engage our emotions of love as we would have for a child or the love for a parent and so on. As human beings, it is easier if we attribute a form and develop a relationship, say, as a father or an all-loving mother, with God. While abstract conceptions and formless states are helpful for some, others find it easier to concentrate, channel their affection and centre errant minds by dwelling on a form of the Infinite Spirit.

There is, however, another reason for attributing forms to the Infinite Spirit. As we noted before, if the Supreme Spirit is indeed infinite in every way, then to declare or avow that He or She or It can only be formless, is to limit the Almighty. As long as there is sincerity of feeling, devotion and pure love towards a particular form, God will assume that form. One of the Gnostic Gospels talks about Jesus proclaiming that he is what you imagine him to be.

Such is the thought behind the many forms of deities, in Hinduism in particular. The acid test, though, of deities such as Krishna, Rama, Shiva, Ganesha, Hanuman not being relegated to the realm of textbook mythology is that through the worship of each one of these so called 'mythological' deities in Hinduism, several individuals have attained enlightenment and have gone on to enlighten others. They succeeded in transcending the relative world, evident through the wisdom and unconditional love those individuals have bestowed on humanity. The Greek gods, such as Zeus, Atlas, Hermes and so on, have, on the other hand, never produced saints that have shone as beacons of wisdom lighting the path for humanity. They are not even worshipped anymore, for there is no eternal kernel of wisdom in their mythologies, no mystical truths.

It must be, then, that the mythological forms in Hinduism have, at their core, some rationale—more than mere rationale: they have at their core wisdom.

Om=Om=Om

Chapter 5

THE GAMBLE THAT
IS MANTRA YOGA

Mantra Yoga Leads to Calmness

It is often said that we are what we think.

If we are depressed, it is because our thinking has assumed a negative context. If we are happy or joyous, it is because our thinking dwells on hope or anticipated pleasure or on pleasure experienced. (Note, though, that such pleasures are always transitory and fleeting, leaving us pining for more and more pleasures of ever-increasing intensity.)

Our true essence, however, what scriptures often refer to as the *Atman*, the soul, remains the same, unaffected, ever a witness. Only our thinking projects a façade that we encase our true selves in, envelop our Atman in. When adverse circumstances present themselves to us (adverse—determined again, by our thinking), calmness under pressure can overcome most problems and hurdles.

Calmness, however, can also be a means of embracing the

heinous and the evil. To think calmly for the good and for spiritual growth is up to us as human beings: a choice that most human beings make. Mantra Yoga helps us not only to think calmly, but also in a manner that leads to the conscious benefit of our individual selves and humanity as a whole.

A calm mind is critical for progress in any endeavour, let alone a spiritual endeavour. It is only a calm mind that can see reality for what it is, just as we can only see the riverbed of a ripple-free river. If the river's surface is agitated, not only does this mar our vision, but the sediment in the river too begins to swirl around. Our minds can be compared to the surface of a river. The greater the stress, the greater the agitation of the mind and the less likely we are to get to know our true selves or to look at problems for what they truly are. Calming the mind is critical, therefore, and Mantra Yoga helps us in this.

We know that chanting mantras benefits us (as individuals) and the rest of humanity—it is not only meant for our own good, but also for the benefit of all mankind, for that alone reflects the highest aspirations of human beings. It is important to note, however, that we begin chanting mantras primarily to benefit ourselves and the rest of humanity secondarily. Before helping others, we must ensure that our own individual needs and wants are met. This should not be construed as selfishness, for it is only when we have helped ourselves to a position of strength that we can be in a position to help others.

To illustrate, flight attendants, when demonstrating the use of the oxygen masks on a flight, repeatedly tell passengers, in an emergency they are to put on the oxygen masks first and only after help children traveling with them. If not, the adult passenger, far more capable of helping a child than the other way around, would be rendered ineffective and children too would suffer. One can rest assured that the flight attendants too will put on their oxygen masks first before helping other passengers, even the elderly, let alone the young and the able, the hale and the hearty.

Similarly, if we do not see to our own needs first and foremost, we would not be capable of helping others. It is only after we have met our needs or transcended them can we look to the needs of others. When Jesus said 'Love thy neighbour as thyself', implicit in this statement is not only that we are to love ourselves, but also that we are to first love ourselves before considering loving our neighbours. If we are not at peace with our own selves, we will love others that much less. If we hate ourselves or we are in a depressed state, loving others would not be possible. If we insist on loving others despite not being at peace within, we would only be worsening our condition, let alone those we are trying to love!

Calmness Leads to an Awakening of the Higher Self or Vice Versa

Since a mantra is infused with power, (at this stage, one has to take this statement on faith—the proof of this can only be known after following the discipline and tenets of Mantra Yoga) chanting with regularity and sincerity awakens that inherent power. The release of energy that follows the regular chanting of a mantra occurs when we chant with sincerity, faith and devotion. The vibrations and the resonance created through such chanting will transform our personalities to one of calmness, to more refined states that carry us finally to the state of enlightenment or Shanti. This power energizes and quickens our aspirations to achieve what we wish to achieve, through the fulfillment of desires that are *Dharmic* (translated loosely as 'righteous', lawful, just) and, more importantly, desires that are aligned closely to our inherent nature. It would be equally correct to say that following the discipline of Mantra Yoga leads to a gradual awakening of the 'higher self', which in turn leads to a state of calmness no matter what circumstances are presented to us. The 'higher self' and a state of calmness are synonymous.

It was the Buddha who said that the only thing an intelligent person should seek to get to know is that which cannot be destroyed by death.

If we look around, everything, whether animate or inanimate, will be destroyed by death. Mountains will crumble, our Sun will fizzle out, every star that we see will die out (or has already died out despite still being visible!), rivers will dry up, buildings will decay and crumble. What will live after we pass on is the eternal spirit within and the peace that we find in the now. Each one of us has a unique gift that is revealed when we attain that sense of peace and calmness. Mantra Yoga then leads us to finding our true selves, our path in life—our Dharma, the pursuit of desires closely aligned to our true nature.

Trust the Process without Reservation

At this early stage, these claims might seem farfetched. As mentioned earlier, faith is required for taking that first step of committing oneself to the process. Faith is not believing without proof, but it is trusting without reservation; there is a subtle difference between these two definitions but one that is significant. 'Not believing without proof' connotes a wholly intellectual pursuit, one that rests on logic and sense perception alone. 'Belief' and 'proof' belong to the realm of knowledge, sense perception, logic—all of the head. 'Trusting without reservation', on the other hand, takes into account the realm of the heart as well as knowledge, logic and the head, for 'trusting without reservation' involves coming to believe after factoring all information that is known, even if there is information out there that is unknown to us. In other words, there is no known cause for mistrust or reservation.

So, trust the process without reservation, for it pays!

The Gambling Gene and Blaise Pascal

As spiritual aspirants, some of us may have a 'gambling gene' (or for that matter several gambling genes) in us. For those of us who do, Blaise Pascal (1623–1662), a French philosopher, offers some insight. Pascal would say that taking that first step on the path of Mantra Yoga is a calculated, well thought out 'gamble'.

To clarify, suppose we spend 20 to 30 minutes chanting mantras every day and it proves pointless with no lasting positive effect in our lives. We learn that enlightenment or the state of Shanti and God are mere fallacies; there is no eternal afterlife in heaven and no eternal damnation either. (For if there is an eternal and heavenly afterlife, then as we have learned from what the relative world constitutes, there has to be eternal damnation.) We would, in effect, have wasted a half an hour every day. Suppose, though, the state of Shanti and

God and an eternal afterlife do exist, then the ramifications of not chanting mantras and spending time in solitude and prayer will be a great loss. For then, we are staring at the prospect of eternal damnation!

So choosing between 'wasting' 20 to 30 minutes in solitude everyday (which has immense value on its own!) and not 'investing' the time for a few moments in solitude chanting mantras every day, should be a slam-dunk, a no-brainer!

Again, Pascal's analogy is offered (only seemingly) tongue-in-cheek, for his insight lends perspective to our choosing to spending time chanting mantras in a state of solitude.

Let us now look ahead and learn some of the possible scientific rationale of chanting mantras on a regular basis.

Om=Om=Om

Chapter 6

MANTRA YOGA MAKES
SCIENTIFIC SENSE

A High School Experiment Lends Perspective

The effect that sound vibrations have on objects placed close by lends perspective to the rationale behind Mantra Yoga and, for this, an experiment involving two tuning forks of the same note or frequency is helpful.

Take one of the tuning forks, strike it on the table. The tuning fork begins to vibrate. Place this vibrating tuning fork vertically next to the other vertical non-vibrating tuning fork by holding the stems of each tuning fork, one in each hand, parallel to each other. So now you have one tuning fork that is vibrating and another that is absolutely still, vertically next to each other. Almost immediately, the two prongs of the tuning fork that are still begin vibrating automatically, seemingly magically. How does this happen?

Sound waves from the vibrating tuning fork activate the atoms and electrons within the non-vibrating tuning fork—both tuning forks are, after all, of the same frequency. The non-vibrating tuning fork magically begins to vibrate. This phenomenon is known as 'sympathetic resonance'.

In real life, when we feel sympathy or empathy towards a fellow human being for whatever reason, we are in tune with the vibrations they are experiencing and our beings vibrate in unison and we sympathize.

In a similar manner, the repetition of a mantra creates resonance even when the mantra is silently repeated in one's own mind. This resonance delves deep into the subconscious, tuning our minds to a state of calmness. This reflects, ultimately, in our personality.

The positive effects of chanting mantras become especially evident when the practice is carried on regularly for a period of time. On a day-to-day basis, however, changes are too subtle to be noticed. Even in the long run, the positive effects and transformation of a personality occurs so gradually that aspirants fail to recognize how much they have changed. One tends to easily forget our earlier states and there are no fixed and ready reference points to compare our minds to when changes do occur. The old mind has been transformed, and unless we are able to keep notes and/or remember the subtle changes in our personalities over a long period of time, we remain largely ignorant of the benefits of Mantra Yoga. To keep track of the subtle changes that have occurred, it would help to maintain a daily journal that details our reactions, our behaviour, our thoughts, our day-to-day activities, all of which reflect our states of mind.

The three factors mentioned that make it difficult for us to keep track of the growth induced through the discipline of Mantra Yoga—the subtle, extremely gradual changes in our personalities; the fact that there are no reference points for comparison and finally the length of period over which these changes occur—seem to limit the practice of Mantra Yoga to a select, patient few and those who desire Shanti, as opposed to power, riches and pleasures as ends in themselves. If the changes wrought through the discipline of Mantra Yoga were immediate and are realized 'yesterday', perhaps, there would be a few more giving the discipline a fair trial. It is the age of 'immediate gratification', after all! But that, sadly, is not the case. It is to be noted that those in the path of Mantra Yoga, those who practise the discipline, do not necessarily shun power, riches and pleasure but they simply view them as mere steps to further growth within, rather than as ends in themselves.

Other Scientific Experiments that Offer Explanation

Several other scientific experiments conducted and well-documented by eminent scientists have tested the effect of sound vibrations on material phenomena. These experiments lend an understanding of the process behind the benefits of Mantra Yoga.

In 1787, the jurist, musician and physicist Ernst Chladni (1756–1829) published *Discoveries Concerning the Theory of Music*. In this and other pioneering works, Chladni laid the foundations for 'acoustics', the science of sound. He demonstrated that sound actually affects physical matter and that vibrations of sounds have the quality of creating geometric patterns. Many scientists after Chladni, such as Nathaniel Bowditch and Jules-Antoine Lissajous (both of them in the nineteenth century), studied the effect of sound on physical matter to prove that sound vibrations alter physical states. Our bodies are physical and the physicality of the body is affected not only by our mental state (itself a vibration), but also by chanting mantras which ultimately will have an effect on our neurological system and therefore our neurological state.

The Experiments of Hans Jenny in 1967

In 1967, the late Hans Jenny, a Swiss doctor, artist and researcher, published a book titled *The Structure and Dynamics of Waves and Vibrations*. He placed various materials like sand, spores, iron filings, water and viscous substances on metal plates and sensitive membranes. When these plates and/or membranes were made to vibrate through the effect of sound, there appeared shapes and motion-patterns. In the several materials used to study the effect of vibrations, the shapes and images formed from such vibrations varied from the perfectly ordered and stationary to those that were evolving, organic and even those that were in motion. Jenny made use of crystal oscillators and an invention of his own, the tonoscope, to set these plates and membranes to vibrate. The tonoscope rendered the effect of the vibrations of the human voice visible (through the patterns that the sand grains and other fine particles formed) directly, without the need for any electronic apparatus. This enabled one to see the physical image of the vowel, tone or song directly. In other words, not only could a melody be heard, but it could also be seen as a shape forming on the vibrating membranes or plates. Jenny called this new area of research 'Cymatics' (pronounced 'ki-mat-ics') from the Greek '*Kyma*', which means 'wave'. Cymatics is, therefore, the study of how sounds, through their vibrations, generate and influence patterns and shapes and affect moving processes in the phenomenal (material) world.

Jenny experimented with the effect of sound vibrations on liquids, iron filings, mercury, gases, viscous liquids and plastic-like substances. He was thus able to study the three-dimensional effect of vibrations. His experiments led him to conclude that there was a unity in the shapes and dynamic developments of the forms arising from vibrations. Sri Swami Sivananda, in the 2014 edition of his book *Japa Yoga*, said that in Jenny's research with the tonoscope, when the vowels of the ancient languages of Hebrew and Sanskrit were pronounced, the fine sand took the shape of the written symbols while the modern languages did not generate the same result. Jenny established that words and symbols have a definite association. They have the power to influence and transform physical reality, to create things through their inherent power and even heal a person afflicted in some way. Sound therapy and the healing power of music is well known. Type in 'Cymatics and Hans Jenny' on YouTube and a number of videos pop up on how to build a simple tonoscope, and the fascinating and intricate patterns generated by various sounds illustrate the science of cymatics. Some patterns generated bring to mind the ancient art of mandalas prevalent in Buddhist and Hindu traditions, reflective of the fact that this universe is the result of complex vibrations, which enlightened sages of yore were aware of.

Jenny noted another interesting phenomenon in his scientific experiments. When he took a vibrating plate (vibrations caused by some regular sound or melody) covered with liquid and tilted it, the liquid did not run off the plate and yield to gravitational influence, but stayed on the plate and continued to develop new shapes. If, however, the sound was turned off, the vibration of the plate stopped and the liquid began to run. If the vibrations were started again, before all of the liquid on the plate was exhausted, the liquid, once again, stopped flowing. This, according to Jenny, was the effect of anti-gravitational qualities created by vibrations. Science has proven that the pull of gravity on our bodies ages us. It is reasonable to extrapolate that mantras, chanted regularly, slow the aging process through their vibrations.

The Phenomenal World

Jenny went on to state that everything we see in the physical and phenomenal world is the result of vibrations, oscillations, pulses, wave motions, pendulum motions, rhythmic courses of events, serial sequences and their effects and actions. Even biological evolution, according to him, was a result of vibrations and the nature of the vibrations determined the ultimate outcome. He was of the opinion that every cell in our bodies had its own frequency and that a number of cells created a new frequency in harmony with the rest, which in its turn possibly formed an organ that also created another new frequency in harmony with the two preceding ones.

The key to understanding how we can heal the body with the help of tones lies in our understanding of how different frequencies influence genes, cells and various structures in the body. There have been many cases where illnesses have been cured by listening to musical sounds. Music or sound therapy is a recognized science, although it will be a while before advances in this branch of science will make it mainstream.

Solids Vibrate at Particular Frequencies

To paraphrase Jenny's thesis, solids, under the right conditions, can move fluidly. A macro example of this could even be a slight tremor of the Earth, or a mild earthquake, you will see that the Earth, at the time of the quake, vibrates—flows like a wave—almost as if it was in a liquid state. When this occurs with a high magnitude, serious destruction follows. The stationary ground beneath our feet is something we take for granted till we experience an earthquake moving the ground as a liquid-like wave. This, once again, proves that certain frequencies of vibrations can alter solid states.

Solidity is an illusion. A form that appears solid is actually created by an underlying vibration and when the frequency, among other aspects, of that vibration changes, it assumes a liquid form. John Beaulieu, in his book titled *Music and Sound in the Healing Arts*, states that physics developed the quantum field theory in an attempt to explain the unity between wave and form. The quantum field is understood as the one true reality, and the particles, forms, waves or motions are only manifestations of that one reality.

The next chapter continues in this vein of looking at the discipline of Mantra Yoga through the lens of scientific rigour.

Om=Om=Om

Chapter 7

... AND MORE SCIENTIFIC SENSE!

An Observation by NASA's Chandra Telescope

NASA released a statement some time ago, stating that the Chandra X-ray Observatory detected sound waves for the first time from a supermassive black hole. In musical terms, the pitch of the sound generated by the black hole is the deepest note ever detected from any object in the universe. The tremendous amount of energy carried by these sound waves has caused, and continues to cause, ripples in the gases filling and issuing forth from the black hole. The statement mentions that these ripples are hundreds of thousands of light years away from the centre of the black hole. This indicates that the sound waves have not only travelled that distance, but also that their vibrations are powerful enough to influence changes that are of cosmic significance, at least to us Earthlings. Till now, NASA scientists had only discovered prodigious amounts of light and heat created by black holes, not sounds. These sound waves, according to one scientist quoted in the statement, may be the key in figuring out how galaxy clusters, the largest structures in the universe, grow.

Previous Chandra observations of galaxy clusters did not shed light on the fact that sound waves had such a marked impact around the atmosphere surrounding black holes.

So, sound vibrations do have an impact around us and within us.

Yet Another Perspective from Swedish Scientists in 2002

Dr Eddie Weitzberg and Dr Jon O.N. Lundberg of the Karolinska Hospital in Stockholm, Sweden, conducted a study on the benefits of humming. Their research concludes that humming allows the exhalation of a greater quantity of air from nasal passages than during normal exhalations. This lowers the risk of sinus infection. Sinuses are air-containing cavities in the skull connected to the nose. Exhaling more air through the nasal passages results in a greater facilitation of air from the sinuses to the nasal passages. This, in turn, helps to ventilate the sinuses, protecting them from developing infections. Most mantras, even when chanted loudly, involve a significant amount of humming. The one-syllable, powerful mantra 'Om', for example, when chanted loudly, ends with a long 'hummmm' at the end.

The Experiments of Mrs Watts Hughes

Now off we ride on a long hum to the late nineteenth century and to Margaret Watts Hughes!

Even though we are now going back in time, Mrs Hughes does deserve a final mention (in this chapter, at least) on the science behind Mantra Yoga.

Not much is known about her personal life and even a *Times* obituary on 20 November 1907 tells us little. Mrs Watts Hughes was originally Welsh and came to London from Wales in the latter half of the nineteenth century as a singer. She married and founded a school for teaching singing to homeless boys, which bloomed into a full-scale boys' home, which she ran for 20 years. She wrote two books: *Voice Figures* (1891) and *The Eidophone Voice Figures* (1904). In her books, she explains how she discovered the Chladni effects accidentally in 1885. Seeking a way to measure the intensity of her singing voice, she devised something akin to a speaking trumpet, with a horizontal, rubber membrane over the trumpet end, which she called the eidophone. She sprinkled sand on the membrane, hoping to measure how high it would jump when she sang into the tube.

In *Voice Figures*, Mrs Watts Hughes relates how, when she would sing into the eidophone, she found that each note assumed a definite and constant shape or geometric pattern. She writes that once, when she was singing, a daisy appeared and disappeared. She tried for many weeks to sing that daisy back before she finally succeeded. She learned that precise inflections of a particular note and the coaxing of an alteration of crescendo and diminuendo made the daisy appear. There were even images of ordinary trees, trees with fruits falling, trees with a foreground of rocks and trees with the sea behind, resembling Japanese landscapes. She notes that in addition to wonderful images and geometric patterns, there were also forms produced by certain sounds that were horrible to behold.

How Are These Observations Relevant to Mantra Yoga?

Do these experiments have any direct relevance to the practice and discipline of Mantra Yoga?

Mantras generate vibrations that have a soothing effect on the mind. Scientific observations prove that the influence of sound vibrations on the creation of this universe was and continues to be critical. If sound waves do, thus, influence the formation of all that we see and feel and touch and smell, then it only seems reasonable that the vibrations created by chanting mantras may well coax our bodies and minds into a harmonic synergy of peace. The neurons in our brains and bodies are delicate enough to almost be energy or spirit and will almost certainly be affected by sound vibrations, just as gases, millions of miles from black holes, are.

Admittedly, though, it would be a tremendous leap of faith, from the information given above, to assume that when we repeat the Shiva Mantra (Om Namaha Shivaya) regularly, sincerely and with devotion, the image of Lord Shiva is indeed formed in the ether, and that when we chant the Ganesha Mantra (*Om Sri Maha Ganapataye Namaha*), the ethereal image of Lord Ganesha manifests and wards off obstacles. However, it is not untrue to say that sincere devotees believe this. The reasons for this become clear later. The presence of these deities as living entities will become more plausible after reading of the power and the abiding presence of, love, purity and devotion in one's heart.

For now, though, assuming that such deities exist in the ethereal form, the more concentrated our minds and sincere our chanting, the more intense will be the image that is formed. A mantra has to be repeated correctly for the deity or the Deva to manifest in one's mind and in the ether. As Mrs Watts Hughes's experiments showed, notes sung with the correct inflection and metre, with a particular pitch and particular inflections, produce pleasing images, that is, particular frequencies of sounds and vibrations produce particular forms. Similarly, mantras chanted correctly can have a salubrious effect on the human mind, brain and constitution.

The Universe, Including Our Nature, Is the Result of Sound Vibrations

In nature, there are infinite variations. Consider the snowflake as an example. Each snowflake is unique and since we have seen that forms are indeed the result of vibrations, the vibration that formed a particular snowflake must also have been unique. With an infinite variety of snowflakes (no two snowflakes are alike), there must be infinite variations in the vibrations that cause them, as well. The Vedas state unequivocally '*Nada Brahman*', which translates to 'This whole universe and indeed God Himself/Herself is a sound vibration'. The universe is referred to by the Vedas as the outer garb of the Infinite Spirit, born of and manifested from a sound vibration. The Supreme Spirit is pure energy in the form of divine and infinite vibrations. Our human body, then, is a unity, a coming together of a multitude of vibrations. If these vibrations are harmonized, our body, mind and intellect will function in harmonious peace.

Mantra Yoga helps in this process.

In the Realm of Spirituality, Only Practice Provides Proof

Thus, Mantra Yoga, followed in a disciplined way, helps in harmonizing our outer lives with our inner lives, leading to a greater level of calmness and peace. Rationalization of this process will have no effect and will be of no practical use until we test the process for ourselves. Unfortunately, in the realm of spirituality, we have to practise the tenets taught, to realize the benefit. Even Einstein's theory of relativity was not accepted before being proven practically. In Mantra Yoga, one can observe the effect chanting mantras has had on individuals who have been practising on a regular basis. Even then, one may not be completely convinced as to the efficacy and the benefits of chanting mantras as one has to have had observed the individual's behaviour and state of mind prior to and after he or she has been practising mantras over a length of time. Practice over a period of time and keeping close track of the state of our own minds gives us ultimate proof.

This is somewhat akin to putting sugar into a cup of tea. After adding the sugar, the tea does not begin to taste sweet until we give the cup of tea a stir. The rationalization process and the information given above are similar to the act of merely adding sugar (without stirring it) into our cups of tea. These thoughts need to be put into practice and stirred within, so that they take hold in our hearts through incessant practice. It is only when our hearts are stirred with the thoughts learned and we practise what is learned, that benefits begin to manifest. Until then, we have merely let it enter through one ear and out through the other.

So, convert the information and knowledge received on

the practice of Mantra Yoga into a verb!

We have mentioned that chanting mantras regularly helps in attaining peace and calmness within. To understand this better and analyse it in greater depth, it is helpful to dissect the different states of our personalities and understand our psyches and their constituent states. This will help us in clearly calibrating our personalities and help us grow from whatever stage we are at. As does Hatha Yoga (in the practise of which we are never forced to stretch ourselves more than what is comfortable for us), Mantra Yoga, too, merely asks that we recognize the state of our minds, in full acceptance, and grow from there. There is no single ideal state to start from. Each one of us is unique and we should learn who and what we are comprised of, so as to aid ourselves in growing from that.

It is this aspect that we look at in the next chapter.

Om=Om=Om

Chapter 8

OUR PERSONALITY AND ITS CONSTITUENTS: SATTVA, RAJAS AND TAMAS

The Three Types of Personalities

Mantra Yoga, as mentioned, helps us graduate to higher realms of thought and ultimately to the state of Shanti. To understand how this is achieved, it is helpful to be aware of the constituent elements of our personality. This chapter explains terms and tools that help in getting to 'know thyself'. These tools are universal in nature and this chapter brings them to the level of conscious acknowledgement, leading to a greater awareness of ourselves. Each one of us is unique and each one must tread the path uniquely suited to our individual mental and physical constitution. Unless we are aware of the states that constitute us, we may be treading a path ill-suited to our needs.

Having said that, let us look at some tools to raise our levels of awareness, tools that help in getting to know ourselves.

A personality—any personality—has three *guna*s

manifesting in varying degrees at any particular time. These traits are: Tamas, Rajas and Sattva. It is said that when a soul is born, it gathers within its folds these traits in varying degrees according to the soul's karma, best suited to quench unfulfilled desires. Granted that there is no way to prove this and if this previous statement seems woolly, even irrational, then let us merely understand what these gunas are. That alone will enable us in getting to know ourselves better.

Tamas, Rajas and Sattva through the Lens of Desire

The three gunas are the different states of the mind at any given point in time and to gain an understanding of them, it is helpful to study them through the lens of desire.

We know that a mind with unfulfilled desires is a mind that is seeking. This need not merely be a selfish seeking; it can be an altruistic seeking, as the desires of a saint are, say, in wanting to help the poor. A desire is a longing within and to fulfil that longing we act.

With this in mind, let us take a specific, concrete desire and study the three personality traits—Sattva, Rajas and Tamas—which will help in understanding how the three gunas interact and make us do what we do. When we understand this, we can use the discipline of Mantra Yoga that much more effectively in helping us transcend to higher planes of thought and attain a state of calmness.

Let us suppose that there is a desire in you to teach Hatha Yoga.

You may initially feel apprehensive about embarking on such a project. It may be that you feel the dread of not being accepted by your students or that you lack initiative and confidence in putting together the structure for the course with a level of proficiency. These inhibiting traits stem from the state of Tamas. When we are unable to follow through because of such negative factors, the mind gets bogged down in a state of inertia and mental weakness.

Tamas is thus characterized by negative tendencies and a Tamasic personality is in a state of inertia arising from fear, sloth, laziness, even anger and jealousy. Those who are unwilling to work towards fulfilling their desires, even though they may have the health of body to do so, exhibit Tamasic tendencies. Desires are lodged in their minds and they would cherish the fulfillment of those desires but they do not act to fulfil them, they hold back, making excuses. It is worthwhile to note that the state of Tamas may be so deeply ingrained that one can be unaware of one's own latent desires. Awareness of one's desires, knowing what one passionately wants to do in life, is given to those who are sufficiently self-aware. So, there are relative gradations even within each guna.

Having explained Tamas, let us explain Rajas.

Suppose over the years of nurturing this desire of wanting to teach Hatha Yoga, you have slowly grown in confidence by associating with others who teach, have learned what it takes to become an instructor and you galvanize yourself into preparing lecture notes, skillfully marketing your workshops in the fervent hope that your classes will be successful. The underlying motive for this desire to teach Hatha Yoga may arise solely from an eagerness to gain name and grow in wealth. Any altruism, such as the need to give the invaluable knowledge in you to benefit humanity, is subordinate to the motive of personal gain—there is an element of selfishness that drives your calling. This is Rajas or a personality characterized by selfish activity. To the extent that your acts are selfish, you have a Rajasic personality. Activities tainted with selfish interest leave us either elated or crestfallen depending on the outcome. A desire to teach Hatha Yoga arising from a desire for personal gain will naturally disappoint, if the project fails. A Rajasic personality, therefore, is a state where emotions and the state of one's mind are ruled by the outcome or results of the activity. The joys or sorrows of a Rajasic personality do not emanate from within; they are dependent on the outcome, on the external result. A Rajasic personality's emotions are governed by the outcome of the work performed. One can sense the palpable passion and attachment to activities in a Rajasic personality. It is that passion and attachment to work that, at times, result in grave consequences when things do not go according to well-laid plans. That is not to say that passion and attachment to work do not help in achieving our goals, but as will be seen later in this chapter, calmness and detachment with that same zest for work will result in greater efficiency by reducing stress.

The state of Sattva is refined. The same desire to teach Hatha Yoga embedded in a Sattvic personality would arise primarily to give of the knowledge of yoga to students so that the students benefit from the teaching. A Sattvic personality does not seek name or fame or even monetary return. Monetary gain, especially undue monetary gain, is not the primary motive of a Sattvic personality. In addition, even though a Sattvic desire to teach Hatha Yoga will necessarily involve the same Rajasic activity in conducting classes, such an activity is done without apprehension of the outcome. If it succeeds, a Sattvic teacher will merely feel that he or she has served as a mere instrument of some higher power. The outcome (success or failure) will be tools for further growth—mentally, emotionally, spiritually and intellectually. A Sattvic personality is not controlled by some external circumstance or event. One's own internal growth as well as the welfare of the 'other' are the prime motivating forces that govern a Sattvic soul. Teaching with an attitude of merely acting as an agent for a higher power, a mere instrument being guided by an unseen hand, is fodder enough for a Sattvic personality.

Sattva, Rajas and Tamas Together Act in Varying Degrees

Any activity that we carry out has varying and intermingling degrees of Sattva, Rajas and Tamas that interlace around the activity; no activity is motivated by one guna alone.

To illustrate, consider this: suppose someone wished to hoodwink you into buying a stone sculpture at a price more than it was worth. That wish to hoodwink you into paying a higher price for the sculpture would stem from Tamas in the seller, as it is an act that is done without faith in the seller's own ability to make an honest living. The shopkeeper's act, though, is also motivated by Rajas, since the shopkeeper is making a living through retail. Taking this a step further, if the shopkeeper succeeds in cheating you and donates a portion of his ill-gotten gains to charitable causes or even uses it to feed his family, his Tamasic/Rajasic act has some Sattva too.

To continue with this example, in another instance, a shopkeeper tries to sell you yet another statue, pricing it more than it is worth and you, the potential buyer, realize that you are being asked to pay an exorbitant price; you react angrily and say, 'You thought you could fool me, huh?!' As you rant and shout at the seller, you wish to embarrass and even humiliate the seller. This trait would be Rajas (since you acted out your grievance) equally interlaced with a coating of Tamas (since you wished to humiliate the shopkeeper). Sattva is also evident in your rant, as you were intelligent enough to figure out and be aware of the shopkeeper's devious intent.

Suppose, in yet another instance, another shopkeeper tries to get you to pay more for an idol. Again, you realize his intentions. In full knowledge of the shopkeeper's crooked intent, you look on with compassion, knowing he is committing a wrong out of a lack of faith in his own ability to live honestly. You forgive him, you smile within; you choose to quietly and calmly tell him of his wrong ways, only so that he himself does not get hurt and hurt others in the process; the fact that he was trying to cheat you personally does not trouble you unduly. In this case, you exhibit traits that are Sattva/Rajas. If you are buying the idol for showing off or if the motive has an element of vanity, then Tamas is inherent in the act.

We see, therefore, that any activity has an intermingling of the three gunas. It should be our aim in life to make Sattva predominant in our actions. Earning money through Tamasic/Rajasic means and giving that money away to charitable causes (because of a smattering of Sattva) does not justify the act. Ends, as we well know, do not justify the means. Yet, there is an element of Sattva in such acts.

When we begin to recognize our individual traits or gunas, we begin to progress in our spiritual lives; we begin to recognize, focus and develop Sattvic aspects in our personality and grow.

Self-awareness, 'knowing thyself', a growing awareness of our internal states helps us grow spiritually, but only if we choose to do so.

To the extent that we are fearful, nervous or lacking in faith, we are Tamasic, which may lead to harming others; to the extent that we are working for personal gain alone, we are Rajasic, and such personal gain can also come at the expense of others and to the extent that we are working purely for the benefit of others, for the benefit of humanity, we are Sattvic.

The Importance of Recognizing Personality Traits

Why is it important to recognize these traits in the context of Mantra Yoga? The aim of Mantra Yoga is to grow in our spiritual life, reach the realm of Shanti. In recognizing the personality traits of Sattva, Rajas, Tamas behind any of our actions, it helps us remain a witness to the motives behind our actions and in consequence to the emotions and thoughts that follow as a reaction to the outcomes.

Remaining a witness is a valuable spiritual tool, enabling us to maintain calm even in the eye of a storm. A witness to an event, say an accident or a football game, remains physically and emotionally at a distance and not as 'involved' in the game or the accident. Witnesses are, for the most part, mere observers, remaining relatively detached, rather than enmeshed in outcomes; when we remain a witness, our minds are unsullied, we are masters of emotion as events unfold to fruition. Imagine remaining a witness to events or acts even when we are the principal players or actors; it would, to say the least, act as a destressor. In an accident, often mental states and the ability to maintain a level of detachment from what is happening physically has saved lives, for it is often the shock of what is happening around and the inability to keep a calm demeanour that kills. If we choose to remain a witness in our day-to-day lives, we are bound to grow in efficiency and remain (relatively) stress-free.

Remaining a witness, by definition, entails a certain distancing from our actions, observing our behaviour, even as we carry out our duties. Remaining a witness is critical if we are to gather continuous feedback, rectify actions that are not taking us closer to our goals and toward our higher states. To be wrapped up in depression to the extent that we cannot for a moment step away and observe our own depressed state indicates an inability to step away and deal with the situation. To illustrate, if we are wearing glasses that are foggy, the world and all that we look at will be fogged up. If we are not aware of, or tend to forget, the fact that we are wearing foggy glasses, we will think the whole world is really what we perceive. If, on the other hand, we treat the spectacles with some cleaning liquid, the world will be seen clearly. To clean the spectacles, though, we must remove the glasses, put some distance between ourselves and our glasses and after due analysis as to the kind of stain, clean it properly. We cannot clean the glasses while wearing them; we need to remove them and look at them from a 'distance'. This is similar to becoming a witness to our emotions and states. If we are depressed, for example, and we journal our thoughts and put them down on paper, we are, in effect, putting distance between our depression and our true personality. We can then clinically examine our thoughts that we have 'poured' out on paper, and analyse the cause for such a state. When we begin to do this, we emerge from our gloom. We are not our emotions, we are not the states we experience; we merely experience them. Just like wearing glasses that are foggy or need cleaning, our states too can be cleansed merely by becoming a witness to the emotions enveloping us. The analogy of foggy glasses is important as it shows that our states are not us. They are something that we wear like a pair of spectacles.

An awareness of one's own traits or gunas and analysing the means to rectify and grow is an essential step to evolving to higher personality levels. 'Know Thyself' is oft quoted in Eastern and Western philosophies. The study of the three gunas is a vital step and a critical tool in this process and it is helpful to bear this in mind as we tread the spiritual path.

The Physical World We See Was Once Mere Thought

Every manmade physical, material object that we see, feel, smell, touch was once upon a time a mere thought in the minds of individuals. Buildings, roads, pizzas, bags, carpets, the whole phenomenal world was once a mere wisp of a thought; these thoughts then worked their ways through time and space through actions manifesting as physical entities.

In the context of Mantra Yoga, every word, every thought has a *Shakti* (the energy that directs our minds to certain states) embedded within. For example, during a meal if someone were to merely mention a gruesome event or a mere word associated with it, we are likely to stop eating. Similarly, if a mere mention was made of the name of our favourite food, our mouths would begin to water. In each case, the mere mention of a word results in a physical manifestation. In the same way, mantras too have their Shakti, their inherent energy, which leads us to calmness, purity, peace; it transports us from the state of Tamas to Rajas and ultimately to Sattva.

Mantras Induce Positive Thought

Mantra Yoga induces positive vibrations. Just as the body requires food, the mind requires regular sustenance in the form of discipline and good thought to help it grow towards love, strength, forgiveness, fearlessness. It is critical to remember that our personalities are never stagnant. They never remain as is, they either evolve to embrace positive traits or careen downward to materialism, greed, ambition, callousness and other negative traits and morbid tendencies leading to unhappiness. In other words, our minds and personalities either evolve to higher planes, becoming more spiritual or our minds careen downward becoming more petty, more insecure, more jealous, more caught up in the material and so on. Upward or downward, one or the other; never stagnant. One of the most effective ways of upward mobility is the regular, sincere and punctual repetition of a chosen mantra; this repetition, over time, creates new grooves in the nervous system, altering personalities for the better.

The Divine Wolf, the Surly Wolf

It is helpful, in this context, to remember the age-old, almost cliched story of the monk with two wolves warring within his psyche.

One wolf is jealous, greedy, surly, lustful, easily angered, selfish, with no concern or thought for others, a brute, not to be tamed (predominantly Tamasic). The other wolf is placid, calm, loving, generous, kind and concerned about the well-being of others.

His subjects asked, 'If the wolves are warring, which wolf wins the battle within, Master?'

The monk replied, 'That depends on which wolf I choose to feed at any particular moment. The wolf I feed more always wins and that is a direct choice I make, whether consciously or unconsciously.'

It is interesting to note that the monk was a witness to the two wolves warring and although he admitted to feeding one or the other, it was a conscious or an unconscious choice, not the act of an automaton. He was witness to his actions.

Practising Mantra Yoga helps us feed the kind, generous, loving wolf within all of us. When we do a Namaste, we are bowing to the divine within the person we are greeting. We all have sparks of divinity and the potential to manifest it. This does not happen automatically; it has to be a conscious choice by feeding the divine wolf within. This is illustrated by a parable:

A boy loved yogurt. He could never get enough of the stuff. He would invariably be refused when he asked for more than his share. This would frustrate him and so he decided to take matters into his own hands and make yogurt for himself whenever he felt the need. He learned from his mother that yogurt was made out of milk. Not waiting to hear any more, he surreptitiously took a bowl of milk from the fridge and, placing it in the middle of his room, sat and stared. His mother found him in his own room, sitting and staring at a bowl of milk.

'What in heaven's name are you up to?' she asked.

'I am waiting for some yogurt to emerge from the bowl of milk.'

Divinity, like yogurt 'in' milk, is within all of us. However, it does not manifest on its own. Just as milk has to be boiled and then cooled to room temperature, to which is added a spoonful of yogurt culture, left overnight in a warm place for the yogurt to finally 'emerge', divinity within all of us has to be manifested through discipline and regular and sincere chanting of mantras. Mantra Yoga is the antidote to the Tamasic wolf within and the perfect fodder for the Sattvic wolf; it is a choice we must make as to which wolf to feed.

A Sattvic personality is a personality that dwells in the now, on the duty at hand, without worrying about the results. It remains a constant witness to emotions and actions, remaining unsullied and always ready to right the wrongs. The importance of detachment that comes from remaining a witness is best illustrated by another story, that of a surgeon and his son.

There was a surgeon, renowned for his skills with the scalpel. Patients would risk waiting that extra month, just so as to be under his trained eye and steady hand. The surgeon had a son who was the apple of his eye. One day, while out mountain biking, the son injured himself and required immediate surgery. His father was informed and he rushed to the operating room, changed quickly into his gown, picked up the scalpel and for the first time, saw his son lying on the operating table and broke down; his mind was agitated, nervous, dwelling not in the 'now' but on his son's condition. His mind refused to remain a witness and was too attached, naturally, to the outcome—saving the life of his son.

When we take to Mantra Yoga on a regular basis, we begin, in effect, to calm our minds. Our consciousness automatically begins to focus on our state of being, begins to observe our actions, becoming a witness to our forays, and once we begin to observe our own states, we are automatically turned into witnesses. If you are witness to your depression, you, the witness, cannot be depressed! A Tamasic individual taking to Mantra Yoga will become aware of desires that he or she has been ignorant of. With continued practice and awareness, ways and means to act on those desires within will manifest. Mantra Yoga performed by Rajasic individuals will help to grow in ideas, confidence and become less 'in-it-for-me alone', allowing duties to be performed more effectively.

Mantra Yoga, practised in any state, carries us to higher planes. If we think thoughts without being consciously aware of them, we will sink deeper into Tamasic states. As mentioned earlier, stagnation or maintaining status quo is never an option. The unattended, untended mind invariably careens downward to deeper levels of Tamas. To rise higher, we need to consciously discipline our minds and rise towards Sattva and divinity.

Mantra Yoga is an efficient tool in this regard. As noted earlier, the process of embarking on a strict discipline of Mantra Yoga may rest, even with all the rationale outlined, initially on a little thing called faith. Faith is critical. A little thing may be a little thing, but faith in a little thing is a powerful antidote to weakness. It enables us to achieve goals that we might not otherwise achieve. Faith transcends reason. It is well known that our brains are capable of far greater achievements than we are led to believe. It is through that hidden power of believing in oneself and faith in tapping that source of unlimited potential that we should take to Mantra Yoga.

Om=Om=Om

Chapter 9

THE CASTE SYSTEM WITHIN THE CONTEXT OF SATTVA, RAJAS AND TAMAS

Mantra Yoga, despite its universality and applicability in all religions (repeating the rosary with the Mother Mary as the deity is a mantra) has its origins in Hinduism, and if there are chinks in Hinduism's armour, our faith in Mantra Yoga as a discipline will not sustain. One of the blemishes prevalent in Hindu thought is the caste system. It is worthwhile to understand the caste system in the context of the three gunas for a deeper understanding of the three gunas—Sattva, Rajas and Tamas. Recall the two wings, that of faith and knowledge, both of which must remain on an even keel if we are to soar to spiritual heights. Explaining the caste system, increasing our understanding and knowledge of how and why the caste system came to be will help keep faith and knowledge on an even keel. It is easy to dismiss a whole system of thought, if parts of it are flawed—and the caste system prevalent today is undoubtedly flawed. If we gained an understanding of why it was 'instituted' and its role in spiritual development, it will lend perspective to the values and ideals of the ancient world, through the lenses of today's worldview.

Thus, an understanding of the caste system—how and why the caste system originated in an era when materialism was less rampant and the importance of spiritual growth was foremost—will go a long way in helping us sustain the discipline of Mantra Yoga.

Caste System Intricately Linked to the State of One's Personality

It is important to understand at the outset that the caste system was based on the state of our personalities. Hinduism outlines four castes that are intricately linked to the three gunas—Sattva, Rajas and Tamas.

Let us first list the four castes before delving deeper into understanding the caste system: Brahmins, Kshatriyas, Vaishyas and Sudras. Now, the calmer the mind, with no hankering for ephemeral pleasures of this world, the higher the caste. The Brahmins, were, on the whole, devoid of selfish desires. In the ancient world, genuine Brahmins, having renounced the pleasures of this world, were a solace to the world-weary, an oasis of peace, offering succour and hope to those driven to frenzy by material goals. It was their lot to serve as a role model, as counsellors to spiritual aspirants.

Next were the Kshatriyas, the warrior class, enjoined with the duty of defending the community; they were not all-renouncing of pleasures as the Brahmins and were allowed to enjoy the pleasures of righteous cause: the pleasures of family life, pleasures that did not impinge on the willingness to sacrifice—even unto death—their lot for the good of the community.

The Vaishyas or the business class came after that. They had the acumen and the intelligence to carry on business and make money. They were primarily carrying on their businesses for themselves and in doing so served the needs of the community. They were not, as a rule, called upon to sacrifice their lot for the good of the community but recall that every activity has relative gradations of Sattva, Rajas and Tamas and if an individual of the Vaishya caste has Sattva predominating, he will by his very nature, be more responsible in conducting his business.

Members of the fourth caste, the Sudras, were the least calm, the least inclined to reason or even identify with the rest of the members of the community. Their faculties of head and heart were least developed; they were unable, at times even to identify their wants and desires.

The four castes, therefore, are a reflection of our state of mind and are not (or should not be) indicative of lineage. However, whenever the label of caste rears its ugly head nowadays, more often than not, it does so on the basis of lineage. This is a corruption in the original intent and the true motive behind the caste system.

Understanding the Caste System through an Illustration

In this exercise to understand the caste system, let us look at a hypothetical example that attempts to explain why an individual might be classified into one of the four castes.

Let us say, for example, that we make a request of an individual sitting directly in front of a projector, blocking the projector's ability to project the film on the screen. A simple enough routine request can be made, one that we often make, asking someone to move from one place to another for various reasons. While making this appeal to the individual to move, we may use logic and rationale in an attempt to make him or her see sense, if the individual is indeed open to reason and is capable of understanding. We might say, 'Mr... you are blocking the light from the projector and you need to move.' Such a request made politely should usually be enough for the individual to see the reason behind such a request, even if made without the customary 'please' and 'thank you'. This kind of a request is a direct appeal to the head.

The appeal could also be made to the heart, instead of the head. 'Please sir, I know this requires some adjustment on your part, but do me a favour and sit elsewhere rather than where you are; you will gain my undying gratitude.' No reason is given, no telling why the request is made but the attitude of gratitude is predominant in the request. This is an appeal to the heart, not to reason and logic.

Obviously, the most effective appeal will address both the head and heart, giving the reason and expressing gratitude.

Oftentimes, however, neither an appeal to the head nor the way of the heart is open; some individuals are unwilling to listen to reason, nor are they open to gratitude and love. If the cause for which the appeal is being made is serious and compliance to the request from that individual is of critical importance, the only route left open is force or threats or by satisfying the individual's greed, like offering money (which is a coarse appeal to the individual's Tamasic needs). We would all agree that the greater the 'force' required in order to make the individual comply with the request, the less evolved the individual is. Hitler's personality, for example, was one that could neither be reasoned with (appealing to the head) nor pleaded with (appealing to the heart). And thus, he was met with the combined strength of the Allied forces, under the supreme command of not a diplomat or a bureaucrat but a full-fledged military general.

The caste system can be perceived as being related to the extent and development of qualities of head and heart in an individual. A Sattvic individual's qualities of head and heart are well developed and an appeal can be made to the head and/ or the heart. A Sattvic individual's interests and interests of the community at large are integrated and there is no conflict between the two. A Rajasic individual can also be appealed to through the head and the heart, but only to the extent that they do not clash with his selfish interests of, say, running a business or maintaining the family. Kshatriyas are willing to sacrifice their lot if their communities are in danger. Vaishyas are not expected to sacrifice their lot for the community. Their qualities of head generally exceed their qualities of heart and because of this, they are less inclined to sacrifice their lot for the good of the community. Since the quality of Rajas predominates in them, they can be better appealed to through their head rather than their heart, that is, getting them to comply mainly by satisfying a need of theirs.

Stress on the Spiritual Rather Than the Material

What is implicit in this explanation is that the caste system remains sustainable only if the members of the community, individually and collectively, are true to themselves about their own states of mind and the qualities of head and heart. Due recognition must be given to those who are more evolved, the Sattvic souls who form part of the Brahmin caste, not necessarily because they were born to Brahmins but because of their higher qualities of head and heart. If homage to truth, even to the point of sacrificing one's own material needs, is absent at the individual and the collective level, the caste system deteriorates and breaks down. Expecting such collective and individual honesty in any community is aiming for the stars, but then again, if ideals are not high, of what use is living?

The caste system has unfortunately become synonymous with one's lineage; it ignores the inherent merit (or demerit) of the individual. In times of yore, one who was not as developed in head and heart and recognized this in all honesty, reaped much benefit by listening to Brahmins without question, for the latter had the welfare of the community at heart. The Brahmins' sincerity and compassion for the human spirit was evident too in keeping the welfare of the community uppermost in all their actions. Since materialism did not influence thinking to as great a degree and since truth was adhered to at the personal and the collective level, the caste system remained sustainable as long as this held true. Moral authority bestowed on Brahmins was not only a recognition by the community of their evolved state but a tribute to the community as a whole in recognizing the gunas of individuals for the spiritual good of the whole.

The caste system breaks down when money and wealth are the goals in life, when wealth becomes the source of power and comfort. If an individual with lesser qualities of head and heart, somehow gains access to wealth, then he questions everything, more than someone who has the larger interests of the community at heart. The system ends up being a free-for-all materialism. The caste system was never meant to accommodate an infrastructure that does not recognize the individual and collective souls' welfare. This is woolly, to say the least. Welfare of the soul can never be quantified, measured and put to objective verification. But imagine a time when it was universally recognized that we human beings are spiritual souls who are passing through a phase where we are enamoured of the pleasures of this world, of the flesh and of wealth. Recognizing that these earthly pleasures are ephemeral and not ends in themselves gives credibility to the caste system. After all, if the aim of life is to develop the love of God or the attainment of a state that transcends the need for pleasures of this world, then the caste system, with each individual assigned a specific role, according to qualities of head and heart inherent in him or her, is just, for our goal is to attain the state of Shanti, whatever our qualities of head and heart are. And the caste system worked well in such an environment.

Many Sages of Yore Were Not of Brahmin Lineage

That many enlightened sages of yore were not born to Brahmin parents is testimony that the original caste system once was sound. Sage Vyasa (the author of the Mahabharata and the Bhagavad Gita), Sage Valmiki (author of the Ramayana) and

Kabirdas (poet-saint) were just a few individuals who were non-Brahmins at birth and yet attained sainthood. These sages were recognized by the hoi polloi for their greatness, their wisdom. There were no diktats issued, no pontiff who beatified sages Vyasa, Valmiki, Vishwamitra; they were recognized as sages, as men of towering intellect and heart by all. When we recognize an individual's spiritual worth despite his low material status, it is a testimony to our own high spiritual status.

Caste System Has Been Misinterpreted

In today's world, with the onset of materialism and the stress on material wealth as an indication of one's status, the caste system breaks down. Material wealth does not restrict itself to those who have higher qualities of head and heart and when a person with little or no qualities of head and heart is rich in wealth and material comfort, he or she is unlikely to listen to a Brahmin for the welfare of the community at large.

'Who is he to advise me?' would be the first question that would come to such a mind. This is far too often illustrated in real life: Josef Stalin, for example, was asked to propitiate the Pope in order to encourage the growth of Catholicism in his country by the then French foreign minister, Pierre Laval. Stalin replied, 'The Pope? How many divisions does he have?' The problem also arises from insincerity on the part of the so-called Brahmins of today, for whom the clutches of materialism have proven all too alluring. A Brahmin with wealth and power is a contradiction in terms, yet it is such wealth and power that garners respect and awe in this day and age. In the great Indian epics of the Ramayana and Mahabharata, *Rakshasas* (individuals with very little qualities of head and heart and with evil intent) somehow acquire immense power, material wealth and stature and seek to impose their own megalomaniacal will on others.

Such individuals have existed in the past, exist today and will continue to manifest in the future.

Expounding on the Caste System—A Digression?

An explanation of the caste system in the context of Mantra Yoga is apt, not a digression. Since Mantra Yoga originated in a part of the world where the caste system is still prevalent, that fact alone might be viewed as a sufficient chink to ignore the benefits arising from practising the discipline of, and the rationale underlying, Mantra Yoga. The perspective offered in this chapter is hopefully sufficient to gloss over the undeniable degradation of the caste system that is presently evident.

Having said that, the discipline of Mantra Yoga is not Eastern or Western; it is not restricted to those who are Hindu or Christian or Buddhist. As great men like Lincoln, Mandela, Buddha and Christ transcend national borders and identities, Mantra Yoga and the philosophy behind it transcends religions and belongs to humanity. For Truth transcends all boundaries; Truth is eternal and Mantra Yoga is a discipline that is true and eternal.

Om=Om=Om

Chapter 10

PURITY

What Is Purity?

The benefits arising from practising Mantra Yoga come in abundance to those who are pure in heart. What is 'purity', seemingly vague, easily slipping into the realm of a well-worn cliché?

'Blessed are the pure of heart, for they shall see God,' said one of whom we all know. And for those who do not know, it was Christ.

What does 'pure of heart' mean?

'Purity of heart' is that attribute that looks to the needs of the other, transcending one's own needs and desires, even transcending one's own wounds and bitterness. It is the ability to love, not for any reason other than love alone. When an act is pure, the motive behind the act is not contrived to benefit the one who acts, there are no hidden agendas. The 'what's-in-it-for-me' syndrome is just not there!

This hearkens back to the Sattvic personality and of the desire to teach Hatha Yoga with that kind of personality. The level of purity of the desire to teach is determined by how much of that desire to teach is there to primarily benefit others. As we have seen, this attribute allows us to pursue goals effectively. The more attached we are to consequences, the more ineffective our actions will be in achieving our goals. Attachment and dwelling on the fruits of our actions, we have seen, are not conducive to actions being performed well. Recall the incident of the surgeon called to operate on his own son.

Question: How does one become pure?

Answer: By practising the discipline of Mantra Yoga.

This may seem paradoxical, even counter-intuitive. Faith is critical to transcend the paradox: believe in it, practise it, reap the benefits. Faith is essential for the practice till benefits are reaped.

And yet that alone does not help in keeping faith and knowledge on an even keel. We need to know how the discipline of Mantra Yoga manifests purity of heart. When we discipline our routine to include an allotted time for solitude and the chanting of mantras, we are giving priority to that which is not of this world, that which is eternal. When we begin to chant mantras on a regular basis, we are recognizing the importance of internal, spiritual growth and the importance of weaning ourselves away from the material world. The practice enables our personalities to experience and live in a cocoon of peace that comes from within, not dependent on what we own or on status symbols that are without.

Consciously Purify

It is true that the disciplined practise of Mantra Yoga leads to purity of heart. But we must also consciously do what we can to purify ourselves in thought, word and deed. If we know we can control our negative vibes or love someone without an ulterior motive or carry out an act without a thought to benefit ourselves, by following through, we are growing in purity.

It is akin to brushing our teeth after a meal. We do not brush our teeth when our mouths are full or partially full of food. We get rid of the food in our palates by initially rinsing our mouths and then brushing to further cleanse our teeth. Making a conscious effort to purify our thoughts and our lives to the extent we are able, only makes common sense.

As we dwell on making an effort to purify our heart, it is instructive to reflect on the words of Mother Teresa: Give until it hurts. Just a little. If in any act of charity or goodwill, the act of giving of our time or our resources does not hurt at least a little, what have we given? If it hurts a little, we are stretching our comfort zones; we are practising the art of giving more of ourselves and renouncing a little pleasure. Over time, giving till it hurts will render immunity to the hurt, till it does not hurt as much as it used to. We must then stretch ourselves further. This is relevant here as the process of purifying ourselves is a process of stretching ourselves till it hurts a little and growing internally each time. Mantra Yoga is a ritual that anchors our being to the spiritual path. It is a constant reminder of the conscious need to purify as well as the discipline of Mantra Yoga acting as a purifier, subconsciously. Purity should be an end goal in itself and it seems logical that Christ spoke so highly of the pure.

The importance of purity is illustrated by another parable similar to the analogy we used of brushing one's teeth after rinsing:

> A man keen to begin the practise of Mantra Yoga went to a sage to request of him a mantra to chant. The sage merely turned away and told him to come back six months later. Swallowing his pride, the man waited for six months and presented himself to the sage again. The sage told him again to come back in another six months. The individual, outwardly unfazed, waited six more months, more resolute than ever, and came back presenting himself to the sage at the appointed time. He was refused yet again! In this manner, the sage refused to entertain his request to initiate the individual with a mantra several times. The man grew progressively more distraught and on his next meeting asked the sage, rather haughtily, why he had been refused on so many occasions.
>
> The sage said: 'You want a mantra from me? Okay, but first cook me some balsam rice.'
>
> In anticipation and with joy, the individual immediately went to work, cooking balsam rice fit for a king. When it was ready, the man, knowing that the sage was accustomed to using only his own bowl for partaking of his daily meals, requested the sage for the bowl, so that he could fill it with the delicious balsam rice. The sage dutifully handed him his bowl filled with decaying pieces of carcass, vile and putrid.
>
> The man reacted angrily.

'Why have you purposely handed me this bowl full of dirt? Do you not want the rice I have lovingly prepared? Truly, I feel all sense of goodness in this world has evaporated.'

'Aha! You will not give me food if my bowl is unclean. How can I give you a mantra when your mind is still impure?'

When purity arises, the power of the Infinite Spirit manifests and speaks through the pure of heart. The words do not merely remain words now. They have taken on a divine energy, a Sakti, that transcends rationale. Those pure of heart become powerhouses of insight and of unconditional love and live in communion with peace and a lightness that is of the spirit world.

Of Purity and Becoming Masters

One of the lofty claims of this book is that it will dwell only on the rational realm, keeping clear of theories and suppositions that cannot be readily verified. However, our very rational thought processes are, once in a while, helped along by analogies and perhaps even insights granted to us in scriptures. Let us dwell on one such insight from the Bhagavad Gita that lend a perspective on the matter at hand.

The Bhagavad Gita states that when we pass on, we float away to rarefied realms in dimensions beyond; we do so carrying our half-baked and unfulfilled desires, including desires that are embedded so deep that we may not be aware of them. The Bhagavad Gita states that having passed on to those rarefied realms, those dimensions beyond, there we remain till such time those desires, clinging like dead albatrosses, drag us back to Earth, hopefully in a form and into circumstances full of potential in fulfilling those desires. While alive, we will have an awareness of desires and consciously pursue those desires in a Rajasic state (a state, remember, where we are attached to the fruits of our actions rather than being the calm observer) and, in all likelihood, add more and new desires as the joy and pride of success will make us want to experience more of the same; the disappointment of failure will spawn the desire to eradicate the sense of failure within. Only in a state of calmness and indifference in the midst of pain and pleasure will enlightenment dawn. It is the Sattvic state of calmness where the motive for any act is primarily to benefit the other rather than oneself that serves as a platform for this dawning. Mantra Yoga helps us achieve that state of calmness through a pure heart, not only to attain enlightenment but also to help in achieving goals that we pursue. The repetition of a mantra generates a great spiritual force, a momentum in the mind that intensifies spiritual impressions.

There are those who may point out that to live life with passion and attachment is characteristic of a good life. True, but desires that lead to experiencing pleasure are good only to the extent that we are not made slaves of that pleasure, for this would be tantamount to being no different to being addicted to a drug. A slave of anything or anyone is not the destiny of humankind; becoming slaves of pleasure renders us incapable of recognizing the value of graduating to higher thought and dimensions where our intellect and emotions are satisfied with eternal values rather than ephemeral will-o'-the-wisp, flash-in-the-pan transitory whims. Having experienced a particular pleasure once or twice or even several times, it is wise to move on to states where we have transcended the need for that pleasure. At the risk of repetition, being in need of something implies a dependency, a slave mentality, and to the extent that we are dependent on pleasures (and the greater the dependency, the greater is our tendency to backbite, bitch, complain, envy, hate, crave morbidly), we do not reside in our higher states and are mere slaves of darker forces. When the need for pleasure holds sway, influencing our decisions and actions, our relations and impressions, we have forsaken our own independence and externalized our power of attorney for happiness. We no longer find our bliss from within but become dependent on an outcome not altogether under our control; our focus remains external and we become slaves to the ephemeral!

Consider an illustration that rationally explains the need to learn from and transcend pleasure. Suppose you are in Grade 8. You work hard and get a lot of pleasure in having passed with distinction. Having experienced that pleasure, would you want to repeat that class so as to gain that same pleasure again, even if it means doing better than the previous year? Usually, most of us would pass on that offer and want to move on to higher grades and greater challenges, having learned and grown from the experience of Grade 8. We will want to use the knowledge gained as a stepping stone to overcoming greater challenges.

To want to experience the pleasure of doing well in Grade 8 again would be akin to the Romans of yore, when much revelry and an ability to gourmandize in banquets was a highly prized trait; in such banquets for the privileged, there were rooms where the revelers would go to disgorge the food ingested, only so as to indulge in the pleasure of having more.

Such, indeed, would be our nature, if once having experienced a certain pleasure we do not march onto realms of more rarefied dimensions, for such indeed is the nature of spiritual growth!

It is possible to slowly detach ourselves from being slaves to pleasure, from looking on pleasure as an end in itself; we should attempt to use pleasure as stepping stones to achieve goals that are wholesome, liberating and not those that are binding. Spiritual growth necessarily recognizes the need to slowly detach and ultimately dispense with pleasures that are ends in themselves. We must strive to maintain that as a goal of life. Only then do we come to experience states of calmness and a state of mind that is Sattvic. Fear and insecurity are inherent in personalities that crave pleasure to sustain them. It is the pure mind—sated and harbouring little selfish motive in its actions—that transcends the need for pleasure. Just as humankind is, for the most part, masters of 'fire' and 'water', we too must become masters of 'pleasure'.

Purity, Mantra Yoga and Oneness

Mantra Yoga helps us realize the transient nature of pleasure and of the futility of experiencing pleasures that bind. Through a disciplined practise of Mantra Yoga, and the constant repetition of one's mantra, our minds begin to look within, introspect and learn more about itself. A pure Sattvic state makes its presence felt to those around with the statements:

I have satiated myself with the pleasures of this world.
I seek and crave no more for myself. I am no more a
beggar in this world of pleasure-seeking minions. Now
all I seek is the welfare of others, so that they too may
rise above the need for pleasure.

In other words, in the context of the analogy given, we have
graduated from Grade 8 and have moved on to Grade 9.

It is in that state that one feels a state of Shanti, of peace
and of stillness within. Wisdom is oneness for it is only when
there is oneness in our thoughts, can there be no selfishness
or evil in our thoughts. Unselfishness or purity is oneness.

Mantra Yoga guides our personalities to the state of Sattva
and ultimately to Shanti.

Om=Om=Om

Chapter 11

LOVE AND DEVOTION

Personality—An Intertwining of Head and Heart

It is well known that the personality of a human being is made up of the rational, thinking side on the one hand and the emotional, compassionate, loving side on the other. These two aspects of the human personality are interconnected. An activity can be taken up for a rational reason or to fulfil some emotional need. Spiritual life, too, can thus be approached from a rational point of view on the one hand and from an emotional point of view on the other. The former, as mentioned earlier, is Jnana Yoga and the latter Bhakti Yoga. (It is true that the motive for any activity is usually a mix of both the rational and the emotional aspects; the differentiation is highlighted here for ease in explaining the two paths in yoga.)

The Gist of the Rational Approach

Before we study the path of love and devotion, it is helpful to understand the gist of the rational approach (Jnana Yoga).

This will help us further distinguish between the two paths and give us greater perspective.

Jnana Yoga maintains that this world is in a state of continuous flux. This is easily observed. At any and every moment, there is a creation–preservation–destruction continuum. All that we see of this world will one day crumble, disintegrate or fizzle out. The Himalayan mountain range, one of the most awe inspiring and magnificent sights nature has to offer, will one day crumble to level dust. Our Sun, which countless generations have taken for granted, will one day exhaust its burning gases. All human relationships will one day be rendered asunder. All that we see, feel, hear and taste will one day come to an unceremonious end. To balance this endgame, creation and preservation occur simultaneously before they too evaporate in the distance of time, only to begin the cycle anew. Bearing this in mind, Jnana Yoga asserts that to get attached to anything of this world is folly. The mind has a tendency to vacillate and attaches itself to things that give us pleasure; the greater the gratification, the greater is our attachment. Our attachments can grow and the object of our attachment may, in time, change or destruct or simply vanish. This leads to misery. Therefore, Jnana Yoga and indeed common sense dictates that if the mind is to dwell on anything (and it does necessarily dwell on and attach itself to something) it should dwell on the changeless—the transcendent, formless Infinite Spirit, which is also the immanent spirit within all life. If we are compelled to perform certain actions, it would be wise on our part to not attach ourselves to the activity or to the consequences of those actions. Performing our duties with an attitude of detachment and a serene acceptance of the outcome, whatever that may be, should be our lot. Desires for the pleasures of this world are desires for things that will one day disappear; the mind should therefore be channelled towards the Infinite Spirit.

The aim of life, according to Jnana Yoga, should be to quench our desires and realize that we must come to rest our minds on the transcendent spirit without and the immanent spirit within—the Infinite Spirit that pervades all creation. Mantra Yoga helps us in getting to know ourselves through introspection, solitude and identifying desires that we feel we cannot do without fulfilling and those that we can. By dealing with the essentials, we can hasten our spiritual progress towards the calmness and peace within, that characterize the Infinite Spirit. This is Jnana Yoga encapsulated.

The Path of Love and Devotion

The path of love and devotion stems from the heart. As per Jnana Yoga, recognizing that attachment to the changeless is the goal of human life. The Infinite Spirit in Bhakti Yoga is depicted as a god with form, a deity in a shape that human beings can relate to, worship, adore, love. If Christ is worshipped in an image painted by Warner Sallman or by Caravaggio, the emotions of our heart are invoked. When Christ is worshipped as the simple figure of the cross, we are appealing to our rational mind. In both paths, however, we are reminding ourselves of the high principles that Christ stood for, the former through love and the latter through teachings that appeal to our intellect. The cross reminds us of his teachings. The picture also does, but we are more inclined to look upon the picture of Christ with love.

Pure love (that is, love which seeks no return) helps the mind to dwell on and attach itself to these God forms. When this occurs, the intensity of the vicissitudes and miseries of this world seem lessened; the mind is tuned to a 'higher', different, changeless plane. Any setbacks we face in this world become less significant. Losing in a game of Monopoly affects children more than us adults. This is so as our minds are tuned to a higher or a different plane, one that we know to be more permanent. The same is true when we turn our minds to focus on that which is changeless.

Rituals and worship are acts that help in making the mind dwell on the Infinite Spirit with a form. Such acts, done with devotion and love, help the mind wean itself away from worldly cares, refreshing and recharging it for further action. A transformation in the personality occurs, leading to calmness and peace within. The stronger the love for a deity with noble qualities that appeal, the more will we be cushioned from the onslaughts of worldly life.

One often finds that the education imparted in schools and colleges is aimed at developing qualities of the head: the abilities to earn money and make a living, ensuring that students are geared for a career and have skills that sustain them at work. It does not, however, teach them how to develop their hearts; it does not teach them the art of compassion or the innate ability that is within all of us to look to the spirit within (rather than the outer world of pleasures) to satisfy our needs. The colour of our skin, the image we portray through our dress and deportment, our mannerisms, our speech, our accent, all seem to play a vital role in how we are perceived by others and how we perceive ourselves. Secular education does not teach us unconditional love or devotion. Yet it is through love and devotion that we become integrated and whole; without love for one and another, we are mere cogs in a wheel, no more than insentient machines driven by some external force, inhabiting a concrete jungle, for perfect concentration of the intellect is easily achieved by exquisite love; exquisite love is achieved by total concentration of the intellect.

Perhaps René Descartes Could Have Said...

René Descartes said, 'I think, therefore I am.' Computers think; they perform intricate complicated calculations of logic. They can boast of 'artificial' intelligence; they have beaten grandmasters in chess and have even found their 'own way' to Mars and to the very edges of our galaxy. They move, they talk to one another and to humans. Yet movement, communication, intelligence are not evidence that life is present in an entity. It does not mean that they are infused with life spirit. They will never feel love for their fellow computers or even love for the fellow human beings who created them, infused them with 'life-giving' software.

We are, therefore, not because we think, but because we feel for one another, love each other and are able to discriminate between what is transitory and what is eternal. Compassion and love are life! Perhaps Descartes should have said, 'I feel, therefore I am.' For if this was not true, we should rightly fear technological advances being made. Deep Blue, an IBM computer, may well have beaten the greatest chess player in the history of the game—Gary Kasparov—but can Deep Blue find compassion for a Gary Kasparov? Can it love another (not so deep) Deep Blue?

All too often, the first and last slices in our loaves of sliced bread get thrown away. It is not always that we are not aware that those last two slices could become crumbs for sparrows and other birds. At times when we do, we may crumble the two slices, collect the crumbs in a brown paper bag and feed the birds. To the extent we feel, without seeking anything in return, we are manifesting our unconditional love and devotion within. To the extent we lack that feeling, we are mere cogs in a wheel.

There Are Tales that Develop the Qualities of the Heart

The Eastern epics—the Ramayana (which translates to Rama's Way) and the Mahabharata—are examples that appeal to the heart; those who read them are usually attracted to the heroic and virtuous deeds depicted in them. Little appeal is made to rational thought in such epics. And yet both Rama and Krishna (heroes of the two epics) were heroic, compassionate and historical figures who stuck to the path of righteousness and truth, despite tremendous adversity. Legends and mythologies have sprung around these figures, however, attributing superhuman acts to them. Sages wrote the epics as a way to develop pure love for these great personalities. The basic storyline has historical truth to it. However, it has been embellished to develop feelings of the heart. When listening to the Ramayana, we should open our hearts and listen and put aside questions of logic, be accepting of some of the impossible tales or the irregular chronology of events.

The Lord of The Rings and the *Harry Potter* series widen our imagination—a very valuable and precious trait. Homer's

Iliad and *Odyssey* are great epics that detail the lives and culture of the ancient Greeks, even giving evidence of heroism and courage. Dante's *Divine Comedy* contains exquisite verses written by a fine craftsman of the highest order. Tales like the Ramayana, however, in addition to widening our imagination and detailing acts of bravery in the highest, most sublime poetic form, infuse us with values of wisdom and love for an ideal that is eternal and very real in the spiritual sense. When these epics are inculcated into and imbibed by children from a young age when they do not harbour questions of logic, the seed that is planted grows and blooms into infusing courage, love and wisdom in adult life. It is the love of the millions who worship and adore Rama that has made him a changeless form of the eternal spirit.

It is with this attitude of devotion that we should chant mantras. If we adopt the Rama Mantra as our own, it is wise to read the Ramayana and infuse our hearts with love for Rama and his mantra. The infusion of love in chanting one's mantra lightens the 'burden' of chanting mantras. If we love what we are doing, whatever activity it may be, the activity will roll forward like a well-oiled wheel. Remember, a mantra is a mantra only because individuals have attained enlightenment through that mantra. A rich imagination is often the refuge of the cheerful in times of downward swings in mood; it is an oasis that quenches disquieting thought, especially when that imagination is grounded in wisdom and practical knowledge. Epics like the Ramayana and the Mahabharata are grounded in wisdom; they expand our minds to planes not restricted to the level of the senses; rising above the senses they help us maintain an even keel and Shanti at all times.

Jnana and Bhakti—The Two Wings of a Spiritual Aspirant

Jnana (rationale and reason) and Bhakti (love and devotion) are equally important, and spiritual aspirants would do well to develop both equally as they quest towards Shanti. Certain individuals are, however, more endowed with emotion and feeling rather than any innate ability to rationalize and reason. It is for these individuals that the path of Bhakti Yoga is suggested. As love and devotion bloom to maturity, the ability to rationalize and reason also blooms. In India, oftentimes janitors, villagers and others who have received no formal education in their lives chant and sing the names of their chosen deities; they do so because they simply love to worship their lord in that fashion; their faith has remained untrammelled by the onset of materialism and intellectual reasoning. The masses thus follow the path of Bhakti Yoga by adoring their respective deities representing the Infinite Spirit; they dwell on heroic and loving actions, contemplate words of strength, fearlessness and wisdom uttered in parables and simple language and so come to love the form/image that is worshipped. They attach themselves to the changeless forms, making it easier for them to cope with the pleasures and pains of human life. When such pure love manifests with rock-solid faith, this love often leads these souls to the highest knowledge and wisdom. Jnana and Bhakti therefore are the two wings of an aspirant; when these two wings sprout, the aspirant flies easily over the problems encountered in this world with a serene and peaceful attitude.

The Power of Love

It was mentioned that Bhakti Yoga leads to the same destination as Jnana Yoga. In India, ordinary, illiterate souls have manifested the highest wisdom. Kalidas, Kabirdas, Valmiki, Tulsidas, to name a few, were graced with the highest wisdom, evident in their writings, poetry, philosophy and plays, despite having no formal education. Valmiki, the saint who authored the Ramayana was an illiterate, notorious dacoit, a highway robber and a murderer, who went by the name of Ratnakar. He came to regret his past after hearing the story of Rama. Noting his sincerity in wanting to turn over a new leaf, he was asked to merely repeat the name of Rama by his guru Narada. Valmiki would not have been able to understand the intellectual processes of discrimination, the rationale of the renunciation of desires, of the eternal wisdom behind attaching one's mind to an Infinite Spirit.

'Spirit?' we might imagine him asking, 'What Spirit? Where can I see or touch or feel this Spirit that you talk of?'

Living in the plane of the senses as he did, he may never have reformed but he understood the power of love. When he learned of the life of Rama, he loved him immediately; loved him to such an extent that that when he was asked to repeat the Rama Mantra, he felt he was unworthy of repeating the name of one who was so pure, so fearless, so righteous in his duties. Sage Narada, noting his sincerity and humility, suggested that he repeat the word 'Ma-Ra' over and over again; this transmutes to the word 'Rama' when repeated continuously. Valmiki was thus able to not only concentrate on the name of Rama, but the Sakti inherent in the mantra also burst forth, enveloping him. Pure love bloomed in Valmiki's heart with such intensity that he was transformed into one of the greatest poet-saints of all time.

Intellectual reasoning can, at times, be a hindrance as pride in one's learning can and often does crop up and become a significant hurdle in attaining the highest states. Also, as pointed out earlier, there comes a stage when the intellect has to let go and realize the insignificance of its own powers.

Love and faith alone, from then on, will be our surest guides.

An Analogy that Proves that Love Works in the Same Way as Rationale

An analogy helps us understand how love for something can lead us to the highest realms.

A young lady, wide-eyed and amiable, who had always cherished the goal of wanting to become a nurse, attended an information session for joining a nursing school. Keen and eager to begin her learning, she was listening to the lead instructor telling the future nurses that at the end of the three years of training, they would be expected to perform the following duties on a daily or as needed basis. He went on to read an impressive list of skills with a view to impressing the incoming class, of the knowledge they would gain if they chose to join the prestigious institute of nursing. He began to read the skills one by one, ticking them off as he read.

- Observe pertinent, abnormal signs and symptoms of patient's condition and take appropriate action.
- Perform pre-operative teaching with patients.

- Demonstrate awareness of patient's concerns and a willingness to address them.
- Gather required data from laboratories, Electrocardiographies (EKGs) and histories and physicals (H&Ps) for patient's chart.
- Maintain a log of reports received and pre-op calls completed.
- Perform phlebotomy for required labs and lead EKG.
- Maintain a calendar for pre-op appointments.
- Review pre-op charts for completeness.
- Arrange for anaesthesia consult when required.
- Perform person-to-person interactive (PPI) teaching and coordinate follow-up with anaesthesia.
- Coordinate anaesthesia review of charts prior to surgery date and follow up on additional orders.
- Document all pertinent messages or communication with patient in patient's chart.
- Avoid and prevent casual discussion of patient's surgery among employees.
- Maintain a high quality of communication with doctor's offices and community agencies.
- Answer phones, take messages and transfer calls when appropriate.
- Maintain question–answer records/audits for nursing director as requested.
- Initiate communication with the nursing direction or post-anesthesia care unit leader in areas that require feedback, follow-up or need to be addressed.
- Promote the maintenance of quality assurance standards in the office.

Other duties as required, such as:

- Gather and respond to any phone messages from pre-operative patients.
- Answer pre-op phone calls, complete assessments and record in log book.
- File pre-op assessments and reports on charts.
- Handle pre-op appointments.
- Assist pre-op area nurses with any problems related to data retrieval for current day's patients.
- Maintain functions of Admissions nurse in his/her absence.

A daunting list for anyone.

To someone who was bright-eyed and perhaps even naive as to what was expected of a nurse, our friend was understandably overwhelmed with all the work she would have to put in and the information she would have to memorize. After all, she thought pensively, she might be in the position of having to save a life. She could not take this lightly. 'Will I be able to be a good nurse, let alone live up to my expectations of wanting to become a Florence Nightingale?'

She left the information session in a hurry, disappointment surging through her with the realization that she might not be cut out, after all, for the intellectual rigour and demands that were required to fulfil her calling. As she mused thus, however, almost in tearful disappointment at finding herself crushed, she realized that she loved caring for the elderly, the sick and the needy. She had always been there for those whom she knew and who were not well or were convalescing. Her heart would lead her to their bedsides, her heart would often teach her kind acts of mercy. She had already learnt so much just from these visits of the heart. She realized that she enjoyed doing what she did and that she would enjoy, nay love, learning all that she had to learn and commit to memory, even if it did take that much longer than others in her class. Reasoning, thus, she decided to go back to another information session, enrol and join a nursing school. And our friend achieved her most cherished goal as she listened to her heart, even though she may not have had the faith or the intellectual grounding to do so.

A pure heart can and does lead us to the highest realms of wisdom. When we begin to love a deity, without intellectual reasoning, all our work is dedicated to Him. We work honestly, justly, caring for our fellow human beings for we dare not hurt our deity. We work simply out of pure love for God, for our loved ones and mankind at large. Our failures we accept as His or Her divine will; we find meaning in life and we grow to the highest intellectual realms of wisdom.

All this is possible through pure love in a pure heart.

Love and Devotion for an Ideal Has a Power of Its Own

Thus, belittling pure love in the hearts of the masses and priding oneself in our intellectual grounding would be folly as pride itself is a major hurdle in the spiritual path. The way of the heart can seem irrational and, at times, even nonsensical. However, if these appeal to the emotions and help develop the emotional side of the human personality, they will automatically develop the intellectual capabilities of human beings. The emotional side has several aspects to its full development. The emotions that stem from the love that a mother shows to her child, or the pure love between a husband and a wife or the genuine respect bordering on affection between a master and a servant or a guru and a disciple are just some of the emotions that need to flow freely. In addition, one's guilt and repressed feelings need to be flushed out and this again can only occur when love flows freely. Without such free flow, the full potential of the human being, intellectually, emotionally and spiritually, will not occur. That is why emotions in an individual need to be tapped in a positive way. One of the ways of doing so is to revel in stories and epics that bring out these emotions from the core of one's being.

Thus, those who follow the path of Bhakti, worshipping their deity, representing the Infinite Spirit in images, singing hymns or bhajans or chanting mantras with pure love, come up smelling like a rose, oftentimes quicker than those who wish to rationalize and reason their way to the Supreme.

Om=Om=Om

Chapter 12

THE DIFFERENT METHODS OF CHANTING MANTRAS: PRACTICAL AIDS IN CHANTING

Before outlining the different methods of chanting mantras, it is important to note that the discipline of Mantra Yoga is more than merely chanting mantras. It is true that the chanting of mantras is a critical aspect, an irreplaceable cog in the wheel of the Mantra Yoga process. We should, however, adopt a holistic approach in our faith, in our thinking and in directing our emotional lives to pursue a spiritual path, distinct from a purely material or hedonistic path. Adopting that spiritual path, to reiterate, entails a recognition that ultimately, we, who are on the path, must internalize the fact that pleasures and pains are mere stepping stones to the state of Shanti; they are not ends in themselves.

Having made that very important point, there are four distinct ways of chanting mantras while pursuing Mantra Yoga. The first way is to chant mentally without moving your lips. Such mental repetition, if done with devotion, concentration and sincerity, is a powerful method. In Sanskrit, such mental repetition is known simply as repetition in the mind or as Manasika Japa. In this method, the mantra is chanted silently in coordination with the breath: concentrating on the breath flowing in, holding for the slightest trace, breathing out repeating the mantra silently, mentally. Concentrate on the flow of breath inward like a cloud of pure white spirit, inhaling positive qualities; breathe out, mentally repeating the mantra.

Loud chanting is Vaikhari Japa. Loud and continuous chanting shuts out all worldly sounds. One advantage of loud chanting is that whenever monotony or boredom or sleep overpower us, it maintains our levels of concentration. Loud chanting may also help us pronounce the mantras correctly.

Repetition in a whisper or humming the mantra is known as Upamsu Japa.

Writing the mantra is Likhita Japa. While writing the chosen mantra, maintaining silence is critical.

It is for individuals to choose Vaikhari Japa, Manasika Japa, Upamsu Japa or Likhita Japa.

A combination of one or more of these disciplines can be adopted at the time chosen for chanting. Whatever the chosen method, the following are suggested guidelines that should be borne in mind. Some of these pointers have already been mentioned and are stressed again to state their importance. This list will, hopefully, also serve as a quick reference guide:

1. Regularity and punctuality is critical. This helps discipline the mind. One of the most important, indeed critical, requirements of Mantra Yoga is the regular chanting of the mantra repeatedly for a set period of time, for

a predetermined number of times and at regularly allotted times every day. Although it can also be chanted whenever and wherever we feel so disposed, chanting at a set time for a pre-determined number of times frees us from expending unnecessary energy thinking about such modalities. Discipline in our outer external lives frees us internally to grow spiritually. To illustrate, in monasteries, monks are made to stick to rigorous and strict schedules to help them conserve their energy and not waste it on superfluous decisions. If we follow a strict regimen in our outer life, our inner life will be free to grow. We do not waste time asking ourselves what to eat and when to pray and what to wear, circumambulating in indecision and leaving our fate to emotions and prevailing feelings of the day. Outer discipline ensures that we keep directing all our energies to growing our internal life, which is what spiritual life is all about. It does not matter if we do not believe in God, but if we are growing in love, tolerance, patience, renunciation, fearlessness and other positive attributes, then we are indeed spiritual. God can be a prop that merely helps us attain the divinity that is already within us.

So, if our outer life is monitored and disciplined, our inner life is full of growth and joy. Our outer lives, including the setbacks we face, will serve as stepping stones to growth and a higher state, carrying us closer to the state of peace and Shanti within. Those who seek joy or pleasures on the outside alone, without catering to their inner needs are at war with themselves, for they are denying their connection to the spirit dwelling within. This is not conducive to one's growth on any front. Discipline is therefore essential and it is suggested that to practise Mantra Yoga, we set aside a certain period of time each day. The aspirant should choose a convenient time. The early mornings are often suggested, only because the mind is fresh and it helps to begin the day in contemplation and reflection.

2. While chanting or writing the mantra, dwell not on worldly thoughts, just for those few minutes.

   Chanting loudly and/or quickly increases your concentration, especially if one is lacking in focus. A practical suggestion related to this is not to commence chanting if you have a pressing duty at hand. If you are feeling hungry, it is better to appease your appetite before commencing Mantra Yoga. It is better, though, to be organized so as to have a chosen time slot for Mantra Yoga free from such calls of the world. That is why early morning chanting is the best time to do so. In addition to the mind being fresh, the world is still at bay.

3. Avoid thoughts that make your mind wander. However, if such thoughts do come, gently coax the mind back to the chanting. There is an analogy that helps. If one is sitting on the banks of a river, and one observes a log of wood floating by or a duck swimming or a boat drifting along, one merely observes and lets the objects flow past. We do not cling to these objects floating by and let them drag us away. In the same way, if we remain witnesses to the thoughts that come to our minds without getting attached to them and letting them drag us away, these thoughts will stop coming, enabling us to concentrate on the chanting. One should not entertain extraneous thoughts despite

the difficulty involved in this process. The Bhagavad Gita specifically states that the mind is indeed difficult to wean away from old habits and thoughts, but it is possible to do so with discipline and concentration.

4. Practise the discipline at a set time every day. Do not resort to chanting tomorrow's quota today or postponing today's session and doing 'double-duty' tomorrow. When your doctor gives you a certain number of pills to take each day at specific intervals, you would not resort to taking a double dose of it to effect a faster cure. Nor, for that matter should you resort to skipping a regular and periodic intake as advised. Similarly, once you decide you will say the mantra for a certain number of times each day and at particular times, try not to veer from that schedule.

5. Do not chant mantras if you know that you need to run an errand immediately after the chanting. This will only keep your mind on the watch and take your mind away from the actual chanting. This is one of the reasons why the ritual of chanting mantras should be done regularly first thing in the morning or at a time when you have no pressing urgency in mind. Bear in mind, though, that a set time every day is important.

6. As mentioned in a previous point, the most effective time to chant mantras is early in the morning or at dusk. Sattva is predominant during these times. Time has been divided into periods when one of the three gunas, Sattva or Rajas or Tamas, predominate, as indicated before. This can be regulated according to our own personal requirements. We may well feel particularly Sattvic in the afternoon and if we choose to chant mantras regularly in the afternoon out of

necessity, then that is just fine. What is important is that we are aware of our individual moods and feelings and chart our own schedule, one that suits our unique personalities. Having said that, regularity, punctuality, sincerity and devotion are critical attributes while chanting mantras. But here again, even if one chants mantras mechanically, without these attributes, it will still be as beneficial as chanting on a regular basis; it will automatically inculcate the attributes of sincerity and devotion over time. Chanting regularly at fixed times will ensure that the mind automatically starts vibrating in the same frequency as the mantras and begins chanting at those fixed times even when we do not feel like doing so. What we would have achieved is to train the mind into chanting at the appointed hours.

7. It is highly advantageous to sit in the same place every day. Do not change places at whim. Also try not to shift and change your posture once you begin chanting your mantra. This only wastes and expends energy in unnecessary ways. A steady poise also helps control the mind and aids in concentration. Just as when one feels down or depressed, we can, by assuming a body posture that reflects confidence and cheerfulness, make ourselves feel better: a steady poise while chanting mantras aids in concentration. Physical posture and mental framework are interconnected.

8. It has been suggested by the sages that we sit facing the north or the east, which increases the efficacy of chanting the mantras. This may have something to do with the Earth's magnetic field. So, if we are facing north, the pictures or aids to induce concentration placed in our shrine will be facing south.

9. A rug, a shawl or a prayer mat of some sort, specifically reserved for the purpose, should be used, on which we should sit. This helps preserve the vibrations that we generate each and every day. We should also use one set of comfortable clothing for chanting. The less we wear while chanting mantras, the better.

10. Invoking the aids of sight, sound, smell will help elevate our moods and minds to a level where chanting mantras become that much more intense and spiritual. For example, if we feel particularly elevated with the smell of certain flowers, then it is suggested we have those flowers before us when we begin chanting. Incense too is a good aid in this respect for some. The sight of nature, in all its grandeur, or the sight of your chosen Lord, who elevates your mind or the sight of any picture that induces peace in one's mind should be kept in the room where the mantra is chanted. The sound of nature such as birds chirping or the sound of water and such other pleasant and peaceful sounds of nature can be used to invoke peace and calmness within. Music is also a good aid.

11. The chanting of the mantras should be started slowly and clearly. If the mind begins to wander, gently remind yourself and bring it back to the site, the sound of the vibrations, the smell of fragrance and the touch of your rug or shawl. This is also an exercise of being in the now.

12. It is helpful to vary the type of chanting. If the mind is straying more than usual, it helps to chant the mantras loudly. If you are feeling at peace, you will be automatically drawn to chanting the mantras within your mind. Variety in chanting the mantras can help in sustaining interest.

13. After each day's session of chanting mantras, do not immediately leave the place. Instead, sit and quietly absorb the peace that you have generated around you. Try and recollect the mood and the circumstances that generated the peace. Note it down in a journal. If you find that the session was not peaceful, even this should be noted down so as to avoid them in the future.

14. Avoid postponing the chanting to another time, another day, even if you are not feeling up to it. Even chanting the mantra mechanically is better than not chanting it at all or postponing it to another day.

15. Initially, when the mind is not trained to sit for long periods, we can begin by sitting for a few minutes each day and slowly increase the minutes as we begin to grow in devotion, faith and love for the mantra. Over time, as we repeat the mantra, our devotion and faith will grow. All that is needed is commitment on our part. It is suggested that a mantra should be chanted 108 times each session. It is, therefore, helpful to know how to keep count of the number of times we chant it. One way to do so is with beads. The eastern beads usually have 108 or 54 beads and so it is easy to keep track. Beads can be, however, cumbersome. They have always to be treated with great respect and looked upon as something sacred to preserve the vibrations generated. There are also other injunctions against using the forefinger for counting the beads. Also, the beads, according to some injunctions, should never be lowered below the navel, all of which can be cumbersome for those who are beginning Mantra Yoga. So, another way is suggested in the Vedas and that is to keep track with the

help of the digits on the fingers. Each finger is divided into three distinct digits. Let each digit represent one bead or one chant of the mantra. If we start by placing our right thumb on the middle digit of the ring finger and go down one digit after one mantra, then go to the lowermost digit on the pinky and travel north with the thumb with every chant of the mantra on the pinky, and then on to the tip of the ring, the tip of the middle and the tip of the index fingers, as we continue our chant, and then down the index finger and then west to the base of the middle finger and up one more digit on the middle, we would have chanted the mantra 12 times.

Having chanted the mantra 12 times (or one full revolution of the right thumb on each of the three digits on the four fingers on the right hand), place your left thumb on the tip of the forefinger. With the second 12 revolutions, let your left thumb come down one digit on the left forefinger. With the third 12 let it come down one digit more. With the fourth let it touch the tip of the middle finger. In this fashion, the left thumb will come to rest finally at the base of the ring finger on the left hand after completing nine revolutions of 12 mantra chants, which will equal a total of 108 chants of the mantra.

This procedure of keeping count may sound crude and even cumbersome, taking our minds away from the actual chanting of the mantra. Over time, with practice though, it becomes second nature. You do not have to carry beads around and if you wish to keep count while mentally chanting mantras in the subway or anywhere else in public without attracting attention, this method is very helpful.

16. It is important that one bears in mind that when one begins to chant mantras and meditate on a regular basis, one may not begin to experience calmness or peace within immediately. Do not be surprised if you begin to experience anger, frustration and other negative vibes that seem to come out in greater fury. The reason for this is easy to understand through an analogy. When we wash a dried out ink pot or a vessel that contained paint and has since gone dry, initially the ink or the paint will come out in greater fury. The more we wash, the more the dried ink or dried paint flushes out. It is only when we persist and continue to wash the pot that the intensity of the paint or the ink being flushed wanes as the container gradually becomes cleaner. In the same manner, when we begin to chant mantras and meditate, initially, our negative vibes will get flushed out and will continue according to our past impressions. We must remember to persist and keep meditating and chanting, till calmness and purity within predominate much more than the negative impressions. To help monitor our progress, in this regard, it is helpful to maintain a journal, which brings us to our final point.

17. Often, the changes that are wrought in our persona are slow and infinitesimal. Only over time do we really notice the difference. By casting our minds back to the way we behaved in certain situations and circumstances in the past and the way we behave in similar situations now, we become aware of our own growth. Oftentimes, however, our minds usually lose their reference points for comparisons, if we do not keep some kind of a record of

our daily activities. So, not completely unrelated to the actual discipline of Mantra Yoga is that we maintain a journal of our daily activities and thoughts, even if it is random and disorganized in the beginning. Journals help us remain a witness to our actions and our lives. When we are witness to our emotions and actions, we are not immersed in that emotion or the result of that action. If we are witness to our upswings or downswings in mood, we are not in that mood and thus maintain an even keel. We are never what we observe. To illustrate, when we wear spectacles, they form part of our face and we are hardly able to see them. We observe the world through them and when we are looking at the world we forget that we are even wearing them. We are one with the spectacles. We are only able to fully observe the spectacles when we remove and observe them, when we are not one with them. In the same manner, when we observe our depressing thoughts, even our happy thoughts, we are not one with those thoughts, but merely intellectually observing those thoughts. When we thus observe our emotions, we are putting a distance between our emotions and our true selves. Thus, we are better able to analyse what went wrong or what it is that brought us to our down-mood or up-mood. The secret of life, if it may be put that way, is to remain a silent witness to all our thoughts and actions, for it is this alone that will help maintain an even keel. Enlightenment is just that: maintaining an even keel, whichever way our fortunes swing. For, if we get carried away when good fortune comes our way, we are equally likely to get carried away when bad times present themselves. This swing of the pendulum is a characteristic trait of the relative world—good–bad, beautiful–ugly, light–dark, rich–poor and so on. For any attribute, there is an equal and opposite attribute, that is characteristic of this relative world. Hovering above these opposites, comprising the relative world, however, is another state characterized by pure silence, a state of peace. When the Buddha was asked whether there was a god, he remained silent. For to admit to a god with certain 'pure' attributes also means the existence of certain 'impure' attributes and thereby admitting to a devil personifying impure attributes. But, as noted before, it is by attaching ourselves to the good or our conception of God that we rise above the opposites or this relative world. Not getting attached to the swing of the pendulum, between the swings of good fortune and misfortune, and not becoming one with these states but remaining a silent witness is the key to life. Being a witness to our thoughts separates us, creates a haven of refuge, an oasis, from which we can calmly observe the happenings around us, and be a witness to its passing on. For pass on, it surely will.

Maintaining a journal of our daily activities, therefore, helps us, in a disciplined way, of becoming a witness to our everyday life. This in turn, over time, will help us reflect even during the day on how we will be putting our day's acts down on paper. That very process of remembering even as we are noting our moods when looking at an event (which we will later record in our journal) will slowly help us become witness to our actions on a minute by minute basis. A calmness will pervade our whole being as we are putting a distance between the results of our actions and ourselves. And it is in calmness that we can enjoy life more, solve its riddles the easier.

Om=Om=Om

Chapter 13

THE DIFFERENT MANTRAS WITH A COMMENTARY ON EACH ONE

A mantra is so intricately intertwined with a deity, so as to be one with it, that the ancient sages treated these mantras with the greatest of reverence. The mantra and the deity are one and the same; the mantra is verily God Himself/Herself. For when a mantra is repeated constantly and with devotion, the deity associated with that particular mantra 'ensouls' the individual during the time the mantra is repeated (See Chapter 8).

It is helpful to bear in mind that all mantras have equal efficacy and potency. It is the level of sincerity and devotion, the regularity and punctuality with which we chant the mantras, that determine their efficacy. Sages who have attained enlightenment through these mantras have in turn benefited humanity through their writings and wisdom (See Chapter 8).

What follows is a list of some mantras and a commentary following each mantra. The mantra will be repeated 12 times just so as to get an indication as to how to repeat it if and when one adopts that particular mantra.

OM

Om

There are three states of consciousness: the waking state, the state of sleep and the dream state. 'Om' also consists of three distinct aspects. The first is 'A' which represents the waking state (representative of the physical plane); the second is 'U', representing the dream state, the mental and astral planes and the world of intelligent spirits and the third, 'M', represents the sleep state and all that is unknown even in one's waking state. Thus, 'Om', and the sound of 'Om' represents all worlds, the known world, the world which borders the known and the unknown and the world of the unknown. Om, therefore, represents the basis of our life, our thought and our intelligence. According to the enlightened sages of yore, it is from this word, Om, that the phenomenal world was projected. The Bible too states that in the beginning was the Word and the Word was with God. And the Word was God.

When we sit for meditation, if we chant 'Om' loudly three or six or 12 times, it drives away all worldly thoughts and removes Vikshepa or the tossing of the mind. Then we should commence chanting our chosen mantra. The vibrations that are set up by the chanting of 'Om' are very powerful. Pronounced correctly, it arouses and transforms every atom in our physical body, setting up new vibrations and conditions and awakening the sleeping power of the body. The Bija-Akshara, as noted before, is the seed letter. It is a very powerful syllable that contains the life-force of the mantra. Every mantra has a Bija-Akshara and the greatest of all the Bija-Aksharas is Om. It contains within itself the other Bija-Aksharas. The letters of the alphabet are only emanations from Om.

There is a possible scientific explanation to the benefits of chanting 'Om'. In the 1960s, Arno Penzias and Robert Wilson, two American scientists, had been using an ultra-sensitive microwave receiving system to study radio emissions from the Milky Way. During their experiments, they found an unexpected radio noise in the background with no obvious explanation. It came from all directions, not any one particular direction. After repeated checks, it appeared to emanate from outside our galaxy. The discovery of this background noise, which until then was unknown to mankind, proved the Big Bang Theory. According to this theory, the universe came into existence with a mighty explosion. Scientists theorized that if this was true, then the echo of that big bang should still be reverberating through time. Penzias and Wilson's findings proved that this background radiation and noise that existed throughout the universe was that echo. The mysterious radio signal and background noise detected was the cosmic radiation vibration that had survived from the very early days of the universe.

How does this relate to chanting mantras and, more specifically, 'Om'? Chanted properly, the sound and vibrations of 'Om' tune into that primal sound and harmonize us with the vibrations of the universe. When we are in harmony with our surroundings, we are seldom at a loss or feel out of sorts physically or mentally. Thus, all that we are doing when we chant 'Om' is tuning our minds at a harmonic level to the vibrations of the universe, and thus to a greater state of awareness. When we hear a wall being drilled, the noise, if unexpected, can be jarring. However, if we begin to concentrate on the noise and listen to the noise, we will realize that noise too is an elongated 'Om'. When we adopt this attitude and respond to jarring and unexpected noises, they do not seem jarring or unexpected anymore, the noise forms one harmonious link in our lives.

'Om' is usually part of most mantras that are chanted. However, chanting it on its own is also powerful as long as we find ourselves comfortable in imagining God as a formless Infinite Spirit. Others find it easier to concentrate on a spirit with a form. This is because when one worships the Supreme Spirit with a form, we worship not that idol, but some particular attributes of the Infinite Supreme Spirit imbued in the form that we worship. We are better able to concentrate on those particular attributes when those attributes reside in a form that we can relate to. In other words, we are able to relate to a form that we can see, touch and feel, one that is imbued with specific attributes that we are especially in need of. Thus, when Hindus worship an image or an idol, they do not worship that idol per se, but worship the spirit within that idol, a spirit endowed with particular attributes such as fearlessness, absolute unconditional love and the attribute of having transcended earthly pleasures and desires.

Oftentimes, we are drawn to a particular form or idol. On analysis, we may discover that the attributes imbued in that form are ones we are particularly drawn to, perhaps because we lack them. Over many millennia, the masses in countries like India have poured their undying affection and love on such forms of the Supreme Spirit as Shiva, Ganesha, Durga, Kali, Hanuman: forms and figures which may seem quite beyond rational to the uninitiated. Within these so called mythological figures or forms, however, there is wisdom and a rational core.

More importantly, when pure love manifests in the mind of even a single soul for a form of his or her choosing, the Supreme Spirit, who is compassion incarnate, is duty bound to take on that form for the sake of its devotees. Thus, when millions in India worship the form of Ganesha, the Supreme Spirit manifests as Ganesha. Ganesha is a very real entity to millions all over the world, and is a very tangible presence in their lives. These forms and images are many thousands of years old literally, even pre-dating Christ's birth. They have survived, while gods in the Greek and Roman pantheons such as Zeus/Jupiter, the god of sky and thunder and king of the gods; Poseidon/Neptune, the god of the seas; Hades/Pluto, the god of the underworld; Hera/Juno, the goddess of marriage and the queen of gods; Apollo/Phoebus, the sun god and the god of music and poetry among others; Heracles/Hercules, the god of strength and many others are mere mythological figures that have fallen by the wayside and are no longer worshipped because they lacked wisdom in their core. Religion in the East is often interwoven in its mountains, rivers and its landmarks. Thus, mountains and rivers, animals and places are hallowed with a sacred aura. Mythology and history freely intertwine with each other. However, mythology has the ability to transcend time and carry within it nuggets of wisdom for posterity.

Thus, when we choose a mantra as our own, we would do well to consider the form that particularly appeals to us. If the attributes of Jesus are particularly appealing to us, we could chant the Hail Mary or other Christian prayers which are as powerful as any that are revealed. If we are particularly enamoured of renunciation and the annihilation of desires within, having perhaps rationalized that desires are the cause of all suffering, then we should keep Lord Shiva in mind and utter his mantra. Even without rationalization, we may be just drawn to the image and form of Shiva for no particular consciously determined reason. If we are enamoured of fearlessness and wish to fulfil our duties despite all odds stacked against us, we might adopt the Rama Mantra.

Before other mantras are outlined, it is worthy to note that there are many mantras and *shlokas* and the list given below is by no means comprehensive.

GANESHA MANTRA

Om Sri Maha Ganapataye Namaha

Ganesha is the elephant-headed god and is actually a form attributed to the symbol 'Om'. In Sanskrit and Tamil (which is one of the oldest known languages in the world) the 'Om' symbol is oftentimes transmuted pictorially to look like a benign and loving elephant. The Ganesha Mantra, when chanted regularly and with devotion, invokes this god. He wards off all obstacles in any endeavour that is undertaken for a good purpose. Ganesha is also worshipped first in any undertaking and before any worship is begun.

SURYA MANTRA

Om Sri Bhaskaraya Namaha

Surya is the sun god. Once again, to worship the Sun as a god may seem medieval and archaic. However, if one concentrates on the attributes bestowed on this god, that of supreme health and well-being and brilliance, these attributes come to us. As one thinks, one becomes. Surya is also worshipped by millions in India with great devotion. The Surya Mantra bestows health, long life, vigour, vitality and brilliance. It removes all diseases of the eye. Enemies can do no harm. The *Aditya Hridayam* is a shloka of 32 couplets and when recited in the early morning, is highly beneficial.

In addition, there is a specific shloka which, in a mere couplet, invokes the glory of Surya. This too can be repeated as a chant several times. This mantra is known as the Surya Gayatri Mantra. It is:

> *Om Bhaskaraaya Vidmahe Mahadhyutikaaraaya*
> *Dheemahi Thann Aadityaha Prachodayaat*

It is suggested that all Surya mantras be repeated in the early morning.

SHIVA MANTRA

> *Om Namaha Shivaya*

As already mentioned, this is the mantra for invoking the grace of Lord Shiva. Shiva is renunciation incarnate, renunciation personified. This mantra, like other mantras, is short and therefore easy to repeat a number of times. Just as we suggested, it is possible, indeed necessary at times, to vary the modes of chanting (loud, in your mind, in a whisper), it is also at times helpful to chant these mantras in a pleasing musical cadence.

One other note for those who do adopt this mantra: Shiva is often worshipped in the form of a symbol, interpreted in the West to be an image of a phallus. This is quite erroneous. The perfectly elliptical image is worshipped as representing the coming together of the formless with form. For those who lean towards imagining God as Formless Infinite, worshipping a figure with arms and legs does nothing for them. However, to concentrate on a point of reference that reminds them of God as Formless Infinite, one needs some image that we can see, touch, feel. The Lingam, as this revered object is known in India, is thus worshipped. It is representative of Shiva, more than any other deity, as it is stripped of all attributes, good or bad, and worshipped as formless. When the Buddha was asked whether God existed, he remained silent, so as to say that there is God meant that that God had all good, indeed the best of all good attributes. When we thus assign the best of all the good attributes to an entity and name Him/Her God, then we automatically are conjuring another image of an entity with all the worst and vile attributes. A good attribute exists only in relation to its opposite. This is the relative world, after all. An attribute cannot exist in a vacuum. Thus, the Buddha, in saying yes to God, would have also been confirming the existence of a devil. The point the Buddha, and indeed Hindu philosophy, makes is that there is a state above all opposites, which is the state of peace. The Lingam represents that state.

RAMA MANTRA

Sri Rama Jaya Rama Jaya Jaya Ram

Or

*Sri Rama Rama Ramethi Ramey Raamey Manoramey
Sahasra Naama Thathullyam Raam Naama Varanane*

Rama's life and deeds are full of heroism in the most trying of circumstances. His spirit infuses us with fearlessness and great Sattva. Rama is Sattva incarnate.

KRISHNA MANTRA

Om Sri Krishnayai Namaha

Lord Krishna is worshipped by millions all over the world. Krishna is often known as the Purna Avatar or the god who incarnated fully with all his powers. There is a rational reason behind this. Human emotion, in its pure state, can express love in five ways. By love in its pure state, we mean love that only looks to the need of the other without expecting any return. The first of these manifestations of pure love is often in evidence in our love for our children. Often, but not always. Second, pure love is manifest sometimes between spouses, as lovers. Or as children, we might harbour pure love for our parents. There can be pure love without any thought of return between friends. And finally, a state of divine peace can also exist between two human souls, a state that even transcends the emotion of love as two souls commune together as one spirit and not two separate entities. Thus, there are five different ways the human emotion or spirit can manifest its divinity. The Krishna Avatar can be loved in all these five ways. His playfulness and childish pranks have often been poetically strung together into the most divine verses by saints and poets. Reading this manifests our love for child Krishna. There have been many women saints who looked upon Krishna as their husband, just as many Christian women saints have looked upon the Christ as their groom. They are manifesting their pure love for the

Christ. The *Gopi*s of Vrindavan were so full of divine fervour for Krishna that their every breath would sing his name and his name alone. This love by the countless women saints of India, even during the time of his incarnation, has often been misinterpreted and Krishna has wrongly been cast as a playboy par excellence. Krishna can be looked upon as our father, as a friend and one that invokes the highest feeling of divine peace in us. Krishna is replete with and is a repository of pure wisdom and, therefore, he is a Jnaani. He is a selfless worker without seeking gain and, therefore, is a Karma Yogi. He is pure love incarnate and, therefore, is a Bhakta of the highest order. He is a mystic par excellence and, therefore, he is a Raja Yogi. Suffice to say, though, that when we study the character of Krishna, we will see that his powers were indeed extraordinary and one that inspires humans to become truly divine.

It is only when we manifest pure love in our lives that we will be able to transcend this world from being beggars of pleasure to one of peace within. It is only then that we can say, 'Thank you, Lord. I have had my fill of the pleasures of this world, let me now give what is rightfully yours and love without seeking not, craving not'. It is only when we reach this state, at least to a relative degree, that we can experience some measure of calmness.

Thus, when we begin to grow in awareness of the Krishna Avatar, we learn that this incarnation is one that can fill every part of our lives, every aspect of our emotion and grow with us as we grow in life. It is for this reason that Lord Krishna, in Hinduism, has been called the Purna Avatar. Thus, any mantra that invokes Lord Krishna (and there are many) will indeed be powerful.

MAHA KALI MANTRA

Om Sri Kalikayai Namaha

The goddess Kali is depicted as wielding an axe-like weapon in one hand, holding a severed head in another hand. The other two hands are with palms facing outwards, assuring devotees of fearlessness and the granting of boons. Her tongue drools with venomous energy. Goddess Kali is thus depicted as awfully fierce, even terrible looking. It is so because if we are in an extremely Tamasic state, fierceness is required to break us from our shackles. Goddess Kali hacks away, quite mercilessly, at our jealousies, our anger, our hates, our weaknesses and our lower Tamasic nature that cause us to commit sin. If you invoke the Kali Mantra, be prepared to shed your lower nature. Change will mean pain, however, but it is pain that cleanses us. We must remember that it is important for us to stay positive and intellectually aware of the process of cleansing that is taking place and grow mentally and spiritually from this process. The Kali Mantra is powerful and Goddess Kali is a very real and even benign presence, if invoked. She is there for our good, only we must be willing to change for the good.

DURGA MANTRA

Om Sri Durgayai Namaha

The repetition of this mantra removes our laziness, our innate tendencies to procrastinate that arise specifically from our Tamasic nature. This in turn produces jealousy and envy when we witness in others the ability to achieve results through their concerted effort. Jealousies and envy taken far are the cause of unproductive, even negative, actions such as addiction to drugs, violence, etc. Removing laziness and an inability to follow through on one's Dharmic or righteous desires is therefore important. Goddess Durga is not only one who helps mortals from dangers and difficulties, she also helps us across the ocean of this relative world to that state where we are above the poles of opposites. Goddess Durga is a very real presence, especially to the people of northeastern India. She is verily regarded as their very own Divine Mother, a very real and powerful presence when invoked.

SARASVATI MANTRA

Om Sri Sarasvatyai Namaha

Repetition of this mantra will bestow wisdom and intelligence and make you a learned person. You will be inspired to compose poems. You will become a scholar.

MAHALAKSHMI MANTRA

Om Sri Mahalaksmyai Namaha

Chanting of this mantra will confer wealth and prosperity. There is no doubt about this. However, in this respect, it is worthy to note one thing. Although it is certain that the repetition of the Mahalakshmi Mantra will bestow wealth and prosperity on the individual chanting it, if purity is lacking, the wealth will slip away and/or may not be utilized for purposes that one intended the wealth for. In this respect, it is helpful for those who chant this mantra to remember that the Divine Mother has three very powerful forms. One is Durga, the second is Sarasvati and the third is Mahalakshmi. The first form of Durga is depicted as very powerful, armed with an array of weapons, usually subduing a demon and also standing on the head of a black buffalo. This form depicts Goddess Durga slaying the lower nature in our selves, our jealousies, our hatred, our bitterness, depicted in the form of the demon. The buffalo depicts our lazy slothful nature that does not realize its full potential. It is this lower nature that both Goddess Durga (and Goddess Kali) seek to bodaciously cut asunder. It is only when our lower nature is erased that purity will manifest. Life is indeed short and the quicker and the more drastically, even violently (metaphorically speaking), we eradicate our lower selves, the quicker we will experience purity and goodness in our lives and affect others positively. It must be borne in mind that when we begin to purify our lives and the impurities wash away, we will experience pain and discomfort. Just as when we wash a bottle slaked with dried up paint, the more we wash, the more of the dry paint comes out. In the same way, our lower nature depicted in the form or jealousies, anger, etc., will come out of our psyches in a great flood. Initially, this will cause some discomfort. We will even feel like giving up meditating and uttering the mantras, but the fact that such pain is manifesting is evidence that the mantra is working. From the pain that we experience, if we persist, we will begin to grow stronger. We must not abandon chanting the mantra just because we may feel greater negative vibes from within. Change comes with some pain. We must be brave enough to bear the pain. In the Bhagavad Gita, it says that the ability to bear suffering and pain for the sake of truth and growth and attaining purity is the foremost quality in the spiritual life. This attribute is known as *Tithiksha* and that great spritual teacher, Shankaracharya, states that without Tithiksha there will be no devotion, purity and love for God. Spiritual life is not for the faint of heart. It is for the heroes of this world who are willing to undergo what it takes to come through.

It is also worth mentioning here that some people are lucky enough to not undergo as much pain as others do to attain purity. The sages say that our previous karma, in this life as well as in previous lives, determines the extent to which we need to cleanse ourselves. As we grow in purity, we get to know ourselves and our innate personality, and we begin to see what is important in our lives and what is not. Each one of us is unique. It is up to each one of us, therefore, to find out what is unique in our personalities. Truly, when Socrates said, 'Know Thyself', he uttered a very wise statement, for without knowing yourself, there is no progress in the spiritual life. This process of cleansing ourselves is the surest way of getting to know ourselves.

The second form of the Divine Mother is Sarasvati, the goddess of learning and wisdom. As soon as purity and goodness lodge themselves firmly within our hearts, knowledge and wisdom just burst forth. It is said in the Bhagavad Gita that just as a womb is covered by the amnion, the mirror by dust and fire by smoke, so too is knowledge and wisdom within us covered by our own impurities and selfish desires. These three analogies also refer to the three states of our personality that we talked of earlier. The Sattvic mind is the purest and therefore is closest to knowledge and wisdom. It is the Sattvic mind that is depicted by the analogy of the fire covered by smoke. The example of the mirror covered by dust is an example of the Rajasic mind that is aware of its desires and actively, even passionately, pursues them. The embryo and the amnion covering it refers to the Tamasic or the denser personality that is full of sloth, laziness and at times is not even aware of the subconscious desires lurking within. When we remove these coverings or impurities within our personality, the clarity and vision that we will enjoy will enable us to move quickly towards our true goals in a way that is also helpful to humanity. In other words, wisdom becomes the driver in our life in this world.

The third form of the Divine Mother, Goddess Mahalakshmi, immediately lodges in one's heart when purity and wisdom are innate in one's personality. Mahalakshmi does not merely refer to material wealth but also to contentment, peace and prosperity in one's spiritual life as well as in one's external life. If this requires material wealth to be put to good use, then it will manifest according to our station in life.

It is in this order that we should pray for wealth to manifest in our lives. First, we should purify our minds, then seek knowledge and wisdom and then finally wealth and prosperity. If we start praying for wealth and that too material wealth before the first two manifest, then wealth will come, no doubt, but it will bring with it misery that we are unable to handle, just as we are unable to use that wealth without wisdom and compassion. Wealth will come, but it may not stay with us for long, only leaving us in a state of greater dejection. Wealth will manifest, but that wealth will invite jealousy and rancour among our friends, which will only make us feel more cynical and lonely as we feel deserted, with no true friends who care. It is not unknown to read of rich individuals who are lonely and lead miserable lives despite much wealth in their lives. Even with much wealth and material prosperity, it has not brought any peace or contentment in their lives. It is wise therefore, to repeat the Durga Mantra and the Kali Mantra before the Sarasvati Mantra and the Mahalakshmi Mantra, that is, aim to become pure and attain wisdom before acquiring or seeking wealth.

MAHA MRITYUNJAYA MANTRA

Om Tryambakam Yajamahe
Sugandhim Pushti Vardhanam
Urvaar Uk Miva Bandanaan
Mrityor Muksheeya Maam Rithaat

This is one of the most powerful mantras and will save us from accidents, cure incurable diseases and protect individuals from calamities, bestowing long life. This mantra is a life-giving mantra, warding off accidents and death by unforeseen circumstances. It has a great curative effect. Diseases pronounced incurable are cured by the repetition of this mantra when chanted with sincerity, faith and devotion. It is a weapon against all diseases. It bestows health (Arogya), long life (Deergha Ayu), peace (Shanti), wealth in all forms (Aishvarya), prosperity (Pushti) and satisfaction (Tushti).

SUBRAHMANYA MANTRA

Om Sri Saravanabhavaya Namaha

This mantra will ward off evil spirits and influences and will cast a protective halo around ones who chant this mantra.

HANUMAN MANTRA

Om Sri Hanumate Namaha

This mantra will bestow victory and strength.

Hanuman is much revered in India and in countries like Indonesia, Malaysia, Cambodia, the Philippines and other Southeast Asian countries where the Ramayana has taken root. Often, this aspect of worshipping a mere monkey is derided by some. However, for those who worship the image of Hanuman, that image is not a stone idol but a *Murti*, an image which has been sacredly imbued with the Infinite Spirit in the form of Hanuman, replete with the characteristic traits of Hanuman. Hanuman's character is indeed wonderful and awe inspiring. Dwelling and meditating on this character will help us grow to be like him, not in the physical sense, but in the spiritual and mental sense. An analogy helps here.

A slogan that is often quoted in the West, even emblazoned on T-shirts, is, 'I want to be like Mike.' The Mike referred to here, is, as we know, Michael Jordan. The slogan does not allude to the hope that we all should want to look like Michael Jordan physically. Most of us can never hope to be blessed with the looks of a Michael Jordan or even hope to play as well as he does. What the slogan alludes to is the fact that we aspire to imbibe Michael Jordan's qualities of dedication, commitment to the profession of basketball, his sacrifice for bettering his game, his willingness to go the extra mile for his team, even if it means sacrificing his personal agenda and his ability to excel in a sport that is extremely demanding even for amateurs. It is a physical game, no doubt, but in the end, it is the mental and spiritual aspect that distinguishes one top professional athlete from another.

So, when we worship Hanuman, we worship his wisdom (or Jnana), his pure devotion to Rama (Bhakti) and his ability to integrate these twin forces in the form of action or karma in the service of his lord. Jnana and Bhakti are rendered redundant if they are not integrated and put to practical use in achieving our goals or in service of humanity.

Hanuman is also a great mystic, a great yogi, a meditator par excellence, one who remains celibate. His mind is devoted to Rama, so there is no room for companionship in his life. He has reached the pinnacle of human development. In exemplifying excellence in wisdom, pure love, action and meditation, Hanuman serves as the best example of yoga or union of all human faculties within to manifest our higher selves. All for a very righteous cause.

The present tense is used in describing Hanuman's qualities. This is because he is alive and present in the dimension that we are living. It is said that when Rama was about to depart the world, he asked Hanuman what he would like for all the devoted service Hanuman had rendered unto Rama, in effect granting Hanuman a boon. Hanuman merely replied that he had no desire for moksha or complete union with God. Hanuman wanted to remain alive and separate from God so that he may continue to love Rama and delight in serving the devotees of Rama. He was granted this boon, and that is why millions of Indians who believe in Hanuman feel he still lives in his subtle body or, as it is known in Sanskrit, his *Sookshma Shareer*.

It is for this reason that millions in India worship, love and adore Hanuman. When one reads the story of the Ramayana, his heroism, his pure love for Rama and Sita and his willingness to carry out his lord's commands at all costs bear testimony to his peerless character. Most of us know that the Ramayana is the story of Rama. When his consort Sita is abducted and taken away forcibly by Ravana and is kept closely guarded by evil women for almost a year, Sita slowly loses all hope of ever seeing her beloved Rama. All her courage is sapped. She even decides to take her own life, so distraught and depressed is she. It is at this time that Hanuman crosses the sea and presents her with the signet ring of Rama and assures her of ultimate victory. This episode, in which Hanuman brings such solace to Sita, is looked upon by many women in the East as hope against the tyranny that they often face in the world. Hanuman, for them, brings hope and victory. The Ramayana is a true story and although it has been embellished over millennia, its spirit remains as unsullied as ever. Hanuman is the crown jewel of the Ramayana. Jesus said, 'If ye have but little faith, ye can move mountains'. Hanuman, during the battle for Sita, does indeed bring a mountain of herbs to save Rama and Laxmana. Hanuman is alive in the hearts of millions of devotees, a very real entity, because of their love for him.

There is a word in the English language relevant here, and that word is 'Numina'. It means the spirit or the driving force or the divine presence residing in a particular kind of object or place. The Romans believed in particular powers that resided in objects that explained their behaviour. For example, Frutesca was the numen (spirit, driving force) of fruit, while Fulgora was the numen of lightning. Mercia was the numen that caused laziness and Maturna was the numen that held couples together. The spirit of manhood was Genius, protector of the head of the family, to name just a few. Frutesca, Mercia, Maturna and Genius and all the other so-called Roman gods, have, like the Greek gods as mentioned before, all fallen by the wayside, for there was not only wisdom lacking in their core, there was also no pure love. However, gods such as Hanuman and others predate these Greek and Roman gods and have stood the test of time only because wisdom and pure love are very deeply ingrained in their philosophy.

Whenever an idol of Hanuman is set up for worship (or for that matter any idol in Hindu temples), elaborate invocations and mantras are chanted, setting up continuous and harmonious divine vibrations, invoking the Supreme Spirit to manifest in that image of Hanuman. Hinduism, with so many 'gods' and such diverse forms of ritualistic worship, seems almost impossible to understand, let alone be accepted, as being a pathway to God. Yet these rituals and worship (Puja) have meaning. That idol is then transformed into a Murti, a sacred and much to be revered image, with the Infinite Spirit now manifest through that image. The Supreme Spirit is duty bound to take the form of Hanuman and his traits because of the pure love present in the devotees.

A monkey god may thus be a mere monkey god. But almighty faith and pure love for a monkey god in one single soul, let alone in millions who harbour that faith and love, make that little monkey god a mighty force to reckon with.

This reminds one of that wonderful parable in which the maid was asked to walk over the river with the help of a magic mantra, written on a parchment, that was given to her by her guru. She succeeded several times and soon began to marvel at the power of the mantra she held in her hand. Curiosity got the better of her and she began to wonder what the mantra was. What were the words? What was the meaning? Who was the God? She opened the parchment to find one word—Rama. 'What?' she thought. 'Only the name of Rama? No magical intonations? No wizardry?'

And so it was that she was never able to cross that river, never walking across it again. Just like that!

GAYATRI MANTRA

Om Bhur Bhuvah Svaha Tat Savitur Varenyam Bhargo
Devasya Dheemahi Dhee Yo Yo Naha Prachodayaat

The Gayatri Mantra is one of the most beloved and oft repeated mantras in India. It is also a mantra that worships the Supreme Spirit in its formless state. Its meaning is this: we meditate on the Supreme Glory who has created the Universe, who is fit to be worshipped, who is the embodiment of wisdom and light, who is the remover of all our weaknesses that cause us to sin. May she enlighten our intellects.

When we chant the Gayatri Mantra, we pray for an intellect to the mother of the Vedas, Goddess Gayatri, to bestow on us a pure Sattvic intellect and personality, which will help us to realize the wisdom within us. In the Gayatri Mantra, there are nine names:

1. Om
2. Bhur
3. Bhuvah
4. Svaha
5. Tat
6. Savitur

7. Varenyam
8. Bhargo
9. Devasya

Through these nine names, the mother of the universe is praised. The word 'Dheemahi' in the mantra signifies worship of or meditation on the lord.

'Dhee Yo Yo Naha Prachodayaat' is a prayer requesting the mother to enlighten our intellect.

This mantra has five pauses: the first pause comes after 'Om'; the second after 'Bhur Bhuvah Svaha'; the third after 'Tat Savitur Varenyam'; the fourth after 'Bhargo Devasya Dheemahi' and the fifth after 'Dhee Yo Yo Naha Prachodayaat'.

The sages say that while chanting this mantra, one should pause a little at each of these five stages. Letting our mind dwell on the silence as we chant helps us to be in the now and also enjoy the effect of the divine vibrations that are created by chanting this mantra.

Savita is the presiding deity of the Gayatri Mantra. Sage Vishwamitra is the presiding rishi of this mantra who first attained enlightenment uttering this mantra. Ideally, this mantra should be chanted three times: first, at the break of dawn; second, as morning becomes afternoon and third, at the time when afternoon breaks into evening. The Gayatri Mantra is prescribed to all of humanity, irrespective of their religion or devotion to a particular deity. It is universal in its nature. The Vedas specifically state this. The essence of the Vedas is verily the Gayatri Mantra.

The Gayatri Mantra destroys our inability to discriminate the real from the unreal and cures a weak intellect and its inability to see things for what they are. It clarifies our vision in approaching all problems and hurdles in life. There is nothing more purifying than the chanting of the Gayatri Mantra. The sages say that its sincere repetition brings the same fruit as the recitation of all the four Vedas. Even if we do not have the time to repeat the mantra 108 times every day, the mere repetition of this mantra sincerely, with the correct intonation and with devotion, three times before all meal times—breakfast, lunch and dinner—brings great benefit. It bestows splendid health, beauty, strength, vigour, vitality, and a magnetic aura to the face.

According to Swami Sivananda, an enlightened sage who passed away in the 1960s, the sages have prayed for all of posterity, blessing us, saying: May Gayatri, the blessed mother of the Vedas, bestow on us right understanding, pure intellect, right conduct and right thinking. May she guide us in all our actions. May she deliver us from our innate weak tendencies that lead us to inappropriate actions. Glory! Glory unto Goddess Gayatri, the creatress, the geneatrix of this universe. Swami Sivananda goes on to state that regular recital of the Gayatri Mantra gradually and subtly unfolds several phenomenal faculties existing within oneself. The subtle powers that are hidden come to the fore and we are able to know several unknown secrets. Our physical body becomes like a radio equipment which receives messages on different frequencies. With the recital of the Gayatri Mantra, all the power centred within our subtle body becomes activated and energized. These power centres are called chakras and each chakra is a centre of tremendous energy, unfolding mysterious powers stage by stage. This potential unfolds and the divine vibrations from the Gayatri Mantra has the desired effect on the chakras and the mind, proportionate to the number of times it is repeated audibly or mentally. This brings spiritual and material benefits.

In Eastern religions, one of the ways of praying to God is to simply recite His several names, names that glorified His Being, His power and compassion, names that described His goodness and magnanimity in rich and imaginative ways. The names of God are considered sacred, making them holy in their own right. They carry a mystical power that transcends reason. It is believed that the power embedded in the names of God does manifest positively in one's life if recited with devotion and faith. The psalms, from which these names have been compiled, are one of the most evocative and soulful prayers of human kind. To recite the varied and compelling names of God embedded in these soulful prayers can be one of the most effective forms of prayer. This is described in detail in the next chapter.

Om=Om=Om

CHAPTER 14

MANTRA YOGA IS NOT EXCLUSIVE TO THE EAST

Chanting mantras as a discipline is not exclusive to one particular religion. The Eastern religions have, however, codified this form of chanting to a daily ritual, a discipline essential for spiritual growth. There are many mantras that are long and drawn out. For example, the Vishnu Sahasranam is a compilation of the 1,000 names and attributes of Lord Vishnu. Similarly, the major deities in Hinduism, including the Divine Mother, Shiva, Ganesha, all have *Sahasranama* (the word means 'one thousand names') shlokas or mantras that are read with fervour and devotion by their votaries.

Prayer is the most important link between us and God or our own higher selves. What better way to praise, spend time with and increase our love and devotion for our higher selves, than by revelling in the power that flows from such names? Spending time in prayer is critical. Even in human relationships, if we wish to love someone, spending time with that someone is necessary. Love for one's niece, for example, will only spring after spending time with her. Time is essential for a loving relationship. Love will not sprout otherwise. Similarly, if we seek to have a loving relationship with God or our higher selves, that fosters peace in our hearts, time must be spent with God or our higher selves. By focusing and dwelling on as well as reciting these attributes in a rich and an imaginative language, pure love will possess our hearts. Peace will reign within. Conflicts will cease without. The world will be viewed through the eyes of harmony.

The Book of Psalms gives ample evidence of the importance of the names of God. They are to be much revered, for they are 'holy and awesome' (Psalm 111:9). The names of God are our one tangible hold on the divine, for not only are His names 'exalted above all things' (Psalm 138:2), but they are also 'near' (Psalm 75:1). They are 'our help' (Psalm 124:8) in times of need and trouble. God Himself 'turns and has mercy on those who love His name' (Psalm 119:132) and 'He preserves our lives for His name's sake' (Psalm 143:11); it is through His name that we are ultimately able to 'trample our foes' (Psalm 44:5). For this reason, we are asked to 'give thanks and praise His name now and forever' (Psalm 100:4) 'from the rising of the sun to the place where it sets' (Psalm 113:3).

In fact, so much importance is placed on His name that even if we forget His many kindnesses and 'give no thought to His miracles', He will still save us for 'His name's sake' (Psalm 106:7–8). He will rescue and protect us merely because we acknowledge His name (Psalm 91:14). If these names are read with reverence, reflecting solemnly on the power of the words rich in imagination and imbued with love, the immensity and the transcendence of the spirit that helped in conceiving these names of the lord touches us too. Those sages who wrote these incredible psalms will be our presiding sages.

It will be seen that some of the names of God from the psalms are negative. This helps us recognize that suffering and pain are an inherent part of life and they are sent so that we may learn from them, grow stronger through them and ultimately transcend them. To disassociate them from God and His attributes would be tantamount to being in denial of life and truth. We must recognize that through all the pain and suffering that life inevitably and undeniably metes out, human beings can transcend any and every form of suffering. If we can learn to continue to recognize this through all the downturns, we would have transcended to the levels human beings are supposed to transcend to.

Om=Om=Om

Chapter 15

CONCLUSION

In the last century, Einstein proved that the energy of a particle is a function of its mass and the speed of light, popularly represented as $E = mc^2$. Even those of us not familiar with physics or the sciences believe in the validity of this. We take Einstein's words as the truth, even if we may not have tested its validity or understood it. Although this may rest on the fact that there are other scientists who have corroborated this equation, it still remains that we, personally, have not tested Einstein's theory. We continue to believe it anyway. Similarly, the sages of yore made statements without seeking any personal gain for themselves. They only ask that you test their theories and statements before rejecting them. It is true that the statements made by sages do not have empirical evidence and so it is harder to believe them. It is difficult to prove something empirically in the spiritual world, for that is its nature. The spirit is above the senses. And yet, the changes wrought on a sage who has reached a degree of enlightenment (there are infinite and varying degrees of enlightenment) are there for all to behold. There is wisdom and a deep calmness that remains unruffled. Others feel the same calmness in the presence of such individuals. Ultimately, though, the test of enlightenment is the unconditional love such sages have for the rest of humanity. This area does not, unfortunately, boast of empirical measures. The sages welcome the testing of their theories. The effect is deep and personal, one that cannot be denied.

If it does not have any beneficial effect, then we should rightfully and indignantly reject their claims. Till we test them, it would be unfair for us to reject them outright.

A parable is apt here to illustrate this. A father had three sons and, wanting to test the mettle of his sons, he sent them up to a mountain top. He asked them to go as high as they possibly could and bring back whatever they felt was precious. The first son climbing up the mountain felt tired and dizzy when he had reached halfway up the mountain. He looked around and saw beautiful and exotic flowers that he plucked and showed them to his father. His father was pleased. His second son went further up, almost to the top, but could not reach the summit. He noticed precious stones and crystals. He pocketed as many as he could and with the heavy load, careened his way back home. His father was pleased. His third son, however, who had reached the summit, did not bring anything back to 'show' his father.

'But Father,' he said with a faraway smile, 'I saw the ocean, lilting and shimmering in the evening Sun.'

Not all that we have and grow from needs to be seen and touched and smelt and bought. Ivan Boesky, the Wall Street financier who gained notoriety for illegal insider trading in the late 1980s to the early 1990s, is reputed to have said, 'Of what use is the Moon, if it cannot be bought and sold'. If we have to reduce all that we can gain to empirical evidence before we 'buy' into it, it is a sad state of affairs. The onset of technology may be good in a lot of ways. It has, however, its share of blame for the decline in the spiritual values of man. With the invention of the motor car came independence and the ability to travel greater distances outside one's towns and villages. The motor car certainly increased commerce and trade and brought about a higher standard of living, but it also discouraged the sense of belonging that prevailed within communities. People got to know less of each other in their own communities and got to know a larger circle of people more superficially. They also got to know themselves less, with the rise in standard of living and the greater emphasis on material wealth. Simplicity was sacrificed for more and better 'things', things that you could see and feel and touch. If you could not do these, then it was not counted to be of value. Most recently, the Internet has, indeed, provided much greater access to a wealth of information as never before. But, again, does it help in getting to know oneself, bonding with community members, raising one's own self-esteem and the contentment factor? Are people any happier after the onset of the Internet age?

Mantra Yoga helps you spend time with yourself in solitude. It is an oasis in which you can spend time with yourself, get to know yourself, be more at peace with yourself. When this occurs, you are at peace with others too and not hankering after ties that are meaningless, ties that make you look higher in society without necessarily making you feel at peace within.

Mantra Yoga is not merely chanting. It is a philosophy in and of itself. It points to the recognition of the attitude one must adopt in striving to tread the spiritual path. The system of attaining a higher realm, the path itself, is sacred. The end result of this higher state must necessarily translate into a feeling of oneness with all humankind. It would be utterly meaningless if it did not translate into genuine love and compassion for fellow human beings and for all life. Mantra Yoga dwells not on the changing aspects of the world but on the changeless spirit that pervades all life and the universe. Mantra Yoga identifies the infinite and indwelling spirit within all human beings as that very changeless reality, and identifying with that is in essence identifying with the common spirit that suffuses all of life. Compassion and love therefore naturally flow. Thus, oneness and commonality are stressed, rather than differences and exclusiveness. Mantra Yoga also appeals to the masses or the community as a whole by systematizing the path and giving them an ability to follow the path.

The sages have stated that once we do begin Mantra Yoga and keep it up in a disciplined manner, peace will reign within, no matter what external circumstances and problems exist.

So, why not believe these sages and go a step further and test their statements out?

What have we to lose?

Om=Om=Om

INDEX